Aviation Elite Units

332nd Fighter Group

Tuskegee Airmen

Aviation Elite Units • 24

OSPREY
PUBLISHING

332nd Fighter Group

Tuskegee Airmen

Chris Bucholtz
Series editor Tony Holmes

Front Cover
On 24 March 1945, the 332nd Fighter Group (FG) earned a Presidential Unit Citation for its outstanding actions during the 1600-mile mission to Berlin. This was the longest round trip made by the Fifteenth Air Force in World War 2, and it saw the 332nd's pilots airborne for eight-and-a-half hours. During the mission, the group's escort relief failed to rendezvous on time, and while putting in 'overtime', its pilots shot down three Me 262 jet fighters. The final one was despatched by 1Lt Roscoe Brown of the 100th FS, who was flying P-51D-15 44-15569 *Bunnie*.

Brown was serving as flight leader when the Me 262s engaged the bombers nearest to him. About 20 jets made runs in small groups against the B-17s, and Brown's attention was initially drawn to a flight of Me 262s heading north just below a formation of Flying Fortresses. As his flight peeled off to attack them, Brown was distracted by a fifth Me 262 'at 24,000 ft, climbing 90 degrees to me, and 2500 ft from me', he later stated in his combat claim report. Brown quickly re-oriented his flight, slipping in below and behind the unsuspecting German jet, and, after closing still further, he pulled up into a 15-degree climb and 'fired three long bursts (at the Me 262) from 2000 ft, and at "eight o'clock" to him'.

Brown's near-zero deflection shots found their mark – a sheet of flame belched from both engines and the Me 262's pilot, Oberleutnant Franz Kulp of JG 7, quickly bailed out of 'Yellow 5'. The wounded Kulp floated down to safety, but his injuries were severe enough to keep him off flying duties for the rest of the war. The jet was Brown's first air-to-air victory, and he would score his second, and final, kill exactly one week later when he destroyed a Bf 109 near Munich (*Cover artwork by Mark Postlethwaite*)

First published in Great Britain in 2007 by Osprey Publishing
Midland House, West Way, Botley, Oxford, OX2 0PH
443 Park Avenue South, New York, NY, 10016, USA
E-mail: info@ospreypublishing.com

ISBN 978 1 84603 044 4

Edited by Tony Holmes
Page design by Tony Truscott
Cover Artwork by Mark Postlethwaite
Aircraft Profiles by Jim Laurier
Index by Alan Thatcher
Originated by PDQ Digital Media Solutions
Printed in China through Bookbuilders

07 08 09 10 11   10 9 8 7 6 5 4 3 2 1

For a catalogue of all books published by Osprey please contact:
NORTH AMERICA
Osprey Direct, C/o Random House Distribution Center,
400 Hahn Road, Westminster, MD 21157
E-mail:info@ospreydirect.com

ALL OTHER REGIONS
Osprey Direct UK, P.O. Box 140 Wellingborough, Northants, NN8 2FA, UK
E-mail: info@ospreydirect.co.uk
www.ospreypublishing.com

ACKNOWLEDGEMENTS
This book is the end result of a huge number of contributions, small and large, made by a wide variety of people from all over the world. I am especially grateful to Bob Iverson, who made a great volume of documentary data available to me, and without whose aid this book would not have been possible. I also want to thank the members of the Silicon Valley Scale Modelers, and especially Mike Burton, whose enthusiasm for the subject drove my initial interest, and Angelo Deogracias, who, for no apparent reason, is prone to breaking into the 99th FS fight song! I also owe my thanks to Josh Davis, Harold Hayes, Frank Ambrose, Lee Mueller, Meredith Goad, Julio Martins, Leonardo Cardarelli Leite, Cleopas Mason, George Cully, Jon Lake and Eddie Creek. Brett Stolle of the National Museum of the USAF was tireless in answering my odd requests for photographs – his efforts are responsible for many of the images in this book. Finally, I send a huge thank you to my fellow members of the William 'Bill' Campbell Chapter of Tuskegee Airmen Inc, and a special note of gratitude to 'Woodie' Spears, Charles McGee and Chuck Dryden for their assistance and friendship. Spending time with heroes like these is a true honour, and they continue to serve as an inspiration long after they ended their flying careers.

CONTENTS

TUSKEGEE

In the late 1930s and early 1940s, America saw itself as a bastion of freedom and equality, especially in light of the horrors that fascism and totalitarianism were visiting upon Asia and Europe at the time. World War 2 pitted the USA against natural opponents – the militaristic Japanese Empire and despotic Nazi Germany. To most American citizens, the war represented a natural conflict between their virtuous way of life and the immorality of their Axis foes.

To the African-American community, however, the notion that World War 2 marked the start of a struggle against violence, discrimination and racial inequity was patently absurd. For many of them, this struggle already defined their lives. Pre-war America was a divided nation, with blacks and whites living in two parallel societies. In the southeast USA, segregation was a way of life, with blacks attending separate schools, using different restrooms and eating in different restaurants from whites. In most situations, the facilities for blacks were inferior to those for whites. These artificial boundaries were enforced by a social structure that all but endorsed violence against those who would seek to transcend it.

In the northeast and west of the USA, these formalised structures did not exist, but discrimination was present in a more random, but equally virulent, form.

In the 1930s, the US Army's treatment of blacks reflected the behaviour of society in general. While black Americans had served in combat, and all-black units had distinguished themselves during the American Civil War, the wars against the Plains Indians, the Spanish-American War and in World War 1, most blacks in uniform were part of 'service units', performing menial labour and maintenance roles. Similarly, in the US Navy, the only rate black sailors could hold was mess attendant.

These attitudes permeated the military from the top down, and officials were not hesitant about putting their opinions into print. Chief of the US Army Air Corps, Maj Gen Hap Arnold, wrote in 1940 that blacks could be useful as unskilled labour 'to perform the duties of post fatigue and as waiters in our messes'. Secretary of War Henry Stimson held a similar view, stating that 'leadership is not embedded in the Negro race'.

Even so, these views did not keep black Americans from aspiring to fly and fight, and in 1939 the door that had been shut began to open. The Civilian Pilot Training Program (CPTP), announced in 1938 by President Franklin D Roosevelt, mandated that 20,000 college students would be trained to fly each year. This legislation excluded black schools and students.

However, in May 1939, as the CPTP was gearing up, barnstormers Chauncey E Spencer and Dale L White embarked on a Chicago-to-Washington, D.C. flight to promote aviation for black Americans. Upon their arrival in the capital, they conducted a meeting with a little-known senator named Harry S Truman. He listened to Spencer and White's concerns and pledged to help. Truman was especially impressed when he saw Spencer and White's beaten-up biplane, and according to a contemporary account in the Chicago *Weekly Defender*, he stated 'If you guys had guts enough to fly that thing from Chicago, I got guts enough to do all I can to help you'.

A short time later, Congress authorised funds for the extension of the CPTP to several predominantly black universities, and for the training of black students at white colleges. The programme was instituted at Howard University, Hampton Institute, North Carolina A&T, West Virginia State and Delaware State. In all, 2700 black pilots would graduate from the CPTP. At the end of its first year, 91 per cent of the black students that enrolled in the course successfully completed the programme – the same rate attained by white students. On 15 October 1939, Tuskegee Institute (a black university in Alabama) was added to the programme.

SMALL BEGINNINGS

At that time, Tuskegee was far from an ideal location. The nearest airport, in Montgomery, was 40 miles away, and by February 1940 it was clear something had to be done to rectify the situation. The institute leased a plot of land and donated $1000 for materials, and students volunteered their labour to build Airport No 1, which had room for just three Piper Cubs. Still, it solved the problem of the commute, and the students made national news when every member of the first CPTP class passed the Civil Aviation Authority written exams.

The success of Tuskegee Institute's CPTP resulted in the approval of a secondary course of instruction for black students from all over the country, which was conducted at the small airfield at the Alabama Polytechnic Institute in Auburn.

Aviation grew quickly at Tuskegee, and in October the institute urged its alumni to contribute toward a goal of $200,000 to build a much larger airfield. It also sought donations from charitable organisations. One of these was the Julius Rosenwald Fund, and that group held its annual meeting at Tuskegee in 1941. One of the fund's board members was Eleanor Roosevelt, the wife of the President.

The idea of black aviators intrigued Mrs Roosevelt so much that she asked to be taken for a flight. After resisting the impassioned pleas of her Secret Service bodyguards to remain on the ground, she went up in a Piper Cub with flight instructor C Alfred 'Chief' Anderson. Shortly after the flight, the fund donated $175,000 to the cause, and Mrs Roosevelt remained a strong backer of the cause of black Americans in aviation for years to come.

Still, the military stuck to its exclusion of black aviators. One flyer trying to gain admittance to the Army Air Corps had his application denied, with the stated reason being that 'the non-existence of a coloured Air Corps unit to which you could be assigned in the event of completion of flying training precludes your training to become a military pilot at this time'.

Although virtually all of the military establishment and most of the civilian leadership still fought to keep black Americans in secondary roles, President Roosevelt, enmeshed in an election and eager to court black voters, issued a policy statement on 9 October 1940 that officially mandated that black Americans would serve in numbers proportionate to their representation in the US population in combat and non-combat roles alike. These included aviation roles.

While the Navy all but ignored these policies, the Army took some halting steps, including the promotion of Benjamin O Davis Snr to brigadier general, making him the first black American to hold flag rank. In December 1940, the Army Air Corps submitted a plan to create an all-black pursuit squadron, and the units required to support it. Still, black aviators had their applications denied by the Army Air Corps for the reason that there were no black units to which they could be assigned. This doubletalk lasted until Howard University CPTB student Yancey Williams sued the Army to force it to admit him as a student pilot. The Army relented, setting its plan for an all-black squadron in motion, and the War Department soon appropriated more than $1 million to build Tuskegee Army Air Field (TAAF).

On 19 July 1941, 11 cadets and one black Army officer were inducted into military aviation training as Class 42-C at Tuskegee. That one officer was Capt Benjamin O Davis Jnr, the son of Brig Gen Davis Snr. These two men were the only black non-chaplain officers in the entire Army at the time.

The younger Davis was already steeled by years of discrimination – at the US Military Academy at West Point, he had been 'silenced' – no one spoke to him outside of official duties during his four years at the academy. His white classmates and superiors issued enough undeserved demerits to Cadet Davis for imaginary infractions to cause his dismissal from the Corps of Cadets, but Commandant of Cadets Lt Col Simon Bolivar Buckner voided half the demerits and Davis graduated.

Since then, Davis been assigned to a series of four undemanding tours teaching Reserve Officer Training Corps classes at black universities. His daily workload consisted of a single 45-minute lecture to students. The Army had made it painfully clear to Davis that it did not want black officers commanding white men.

Davis applied for flight training and was denied during his final year at West Point, but when the Army initiated its plans for an all-black unit, he was an obvious choice for its commander. The white hierarchy, however,

Capt Benjamin O Davis (right) receives the first batch of students to arrive for flight training at Tuskegee – his classmates in Class 42-C. Prior to this assignment, Davis had been a training course instructor for college reserve officers (*National Museum of the United States Air Force*)

did not abandon its efforts to exclude him. When he took his initial flight physical at Fort Riley, Kansas, 'The flight surgeon who gave me the exam did what all flight surgeons were doing when they had black applicants', Davis recalled. 'He wrote down that I had epilepsy, and I was not qualified for flying training'. The Army Air Force immediately flew Davis to Maxwell Army Air Base in Alabama, where a second physical reversed the findings of the first. With that, Davis was on his way to Tuskegee.

While Davis was a natural choice for CO of the 99th Fighter Squadron (FS), he was not a natural pilot. Indeed, his primary instructor, Tuskegee Director of Instruction Noel Parrish, had to spend extra time with Davis to raise his skills as an aviator to an acceptable level. However, Davis was well equipped with requisite leadership skills that he would soon display in combat, both with the Germans and with the hierarchy of the Army.

Vultee BT-13 'Vibrators' await their students on the flightline at TAAF in 1942. The TU prefix to the numbers applied to the fuselages of both BT-13s indicated a Tuskegee-based aircraft (*Lt Col Harold C Hayes Collection*)

FLYING TRAINING

Students were given primary instructions in Stearman PT-17s, flying from Moton Field. When they had mastered the biplane, the students travelled 12 miles to the still-under-construction base at TAAF and trained in the Vultee BT-13 – an all-metal fixed-gear monoplane widely known as the 'Vibrator'. Finally, advanced training was conducted in AT-6 Texans.

Life for the first students at the base was difficult. Living quarters consisted of tents, and the mess hall was a wooden building with a dirt floor. When it rained, the inevitable result was mud inside and out. It was not this way for all personnel on base, however, as white servicemen dined in a mess hall, complete with tablecloths and uniformed black waitresses. Even as the base buildings were completed, segregation remained a way of life.

This was all but guaranteed when Maj James Ellison, the base's first commander and an ardent supporter of the project, was transferred after an incident in the town of Tuskegee in which a black military policeman tried to take custody of a black enlisted man under arrest in the town jail.

A meeting of the strong personalities at TAAF in mid-1942. Col Frederick von Kimble (second from left in the second row), Lt Col Noel Parrish (third from left in the first row) and Capt Benjamin O Davis (stood to von Kimble's right in field pack and steel pot helmet) (*Lt Col Harold C Hayes Collection*)

After the MP and his driver were also arrested, Ellison intervened and succeeded in winning their release.

The white residents of Tuskegee were already furious about the nearby 'armed Negroes', and because of this incident Ellison was relieved and replaced by Col Frederick von Kimble. The latter individual promptly had the base's facilities segregated, with signs designating them for either 'coloured' or 'white' use. Davis described the air base as 'a prison camp', and other students confessed to being frightened of the prevailing racial climate even while on base.

Von Kimble harboured the belief that blacks had no ability to lead, and was alleged to have told other officers that no black would rise above the rank of captain as long as he was in command. Following an under-cover investigation by the War Department into von Kimble's conduct, he was replaced by Davis' former instructor, Col Noel Parrish, on 26 December 1942.

Parrish was the son of a southern minister, and at 33, he looked far younger than his years. But unlike von Kimble and most of the USAAF

Noel Parrish (right), seen laughing at a social event in this photograph, took over from von Kimble and immediately took steps to demonstrate to the cadets that he would not hold their race against them. Parrish joined the black officers' club and attempted to ease tensions between the base and the town (*Lt Col Harold C Hayes Collection*)

hierarchy, Parrish was fully committed to the success of the 'Tuskegee Experiment'. He served to moderate tensions between the town and the base, and while he was unable to completely eradicate segregation on base, he made immense efforts to demonstrate his devotion to his men.

Upon his assumption of command, the men noticed that many of the signs designed to enforce segregation had been removed. Parrish declined to replace them. He joined the black officers' club, arranged morale-building visits from Lena Horne, Joe Louis, Ella Fitzgerald, Louis Armstrong and others, and ran interference for his men with Washington officials who wanted the training programme ended. As a result, Parrish was widely respected by his students.

'Parrish is the man who proved that blacks could fly an aeroplane', Davis said. In those days, 'To whites, blacks couldn't do anything very well, except dance and sing. Blacks supposedly couldn't fly aeroplanes because that was too technical, and Parrish proved they could. He held the future of blacks in the Army Air Corps in his own hot little hands. Anybody, everybody should be extremely grateful to Parrish for his performance of duty. He wasn't doing anybody any favours – he was performing his duty conscientiously in a way that benefitted everybody, to include the United States Army Air Force'.

CLASS GRADUATION

On 7 March 1942, Class 42-C graduated from flight school at TAAF. Of the original 12 students, five had successfully completed the course – 2Lts Lemuel R Custis, Charles DeBow, George S Roberts and Mac Ross, as well as Capt Benjamin O Davis. These men were the first officers of what would become the 99th FS, and they typified the quality of the officers who would take the squadron to war. Custis had been the first black police officer in the state of Connecticut, DeBow had attended Hampton

Cadets learned on an assortment of second-line types, including P-39s and P-40s. Ironically, these were the first types many of them would actually fly in combat (*Lt Col Harold C Hayes Collection*)

11

A young 2Lt Luke Weathers (far right) discusses with fellow trainee pilots the route for their next flight. This posed photograph was taken at TAAF in late 1942 (*via Jon Lake*)

TAAF graduated 1030 aviators, including 40 who went to the Pacific to serve as liaison pilots. These men survived training in worn-out fighters, like the P-40 in the background of this awkwardly-staged photograph (*Lt Col Harold C Hayes Collection*)

Institute and 'Spanky' Roberts (so dubbed because of his threat to paddle upperclassmen at his fraternity) and Ross had been classmates at West Virginia State College.

As additional classes arrived and graduated, the base received some older P-39s and P-40s for advanced training. The number of men

winning their wings crept up slowly, with Charles Dryden, Sidney Brooks and Clarence Jamison graduating in the second class, and Lee Rayford, Bernard Knighten, Sherman White and George Knox receiving their wings in the third class.

For the students who washed out, there were no other aviation roles to fill – they suffered the humiliation of becoming a private in one of Tuskegee's service battalions. 'You would start out with a large group, and one by one the fellows would disappear', remembered Samuel Curtis, a member of Class 43-G. 'They would go down to the 318th Air Base Squadron, where all the washed-out went to be reassigned – when a fellow was washed out, it was a crushing experience'.

Col Parrish, seeing the high washout rate, ordered that class 42-F should be made up entirely of CPTP graduates, who would be allowed to skip pre-flight and primary training. The graduates of the class included Louis Purnell, Spann Watson, Charles Hall, Willie Ashley, Allen Lane, Graham 'Peepsight' Smith, Herbert 'Bud' Clark, Paul Mitchell, Faythe McGinnis, Erwin Lawrence, George Bolling and Herbert Carter, along with William 'Bill' Campbell and James Wiley, who had been instructors for the previous classes.

Sadly, McGinnis would become the first graduate to die. On the day of his wedding, he volunteered to become the last pilot in an eight-ship formation. The formation went into a loop, and because he had blacked out in the loop or a misjudged his altitude, McGinnis flew into the ground.

The students were also plagued by their weary P-40s, which Charles Dryden described as 'flying coffins'. Mac Ross had to bail out of his P-40 during his first flight in the fighter, the aircraft slamming into a yard behind a shantytown near the base. A short while later, cadet Jerome Edwards was killed when the engine in his Warhawk quit on take-off and the fighter careened into trees.

Tuskegee's fifth class added Walter Lawson, John Rogers, Leon Roberts, Richard C Davis, Willie Fuller, Cassius Harris and Earl King to

Cassius Harris shouts words of encouragement to fellow cadets Willie Fuller and John McClure in their AT-6 Texan in July 1942. Harris and Fuller would go on to be original members of the 99th FS (*Lt Col Harold C Hayes Collection*)

the ranks of the 99th. Lawson survived a close call during training when the aircraft he was flying with fellow cadet Richard Dawson crashed while the latter was trying to fly under a bridge. Dawson was killed, but the dazed Lawson was found walking away from the crash, earning him the nickname 'Ghost'.

With the graduation of Class 42-G in July 1942, the squadron was finally at full strength. Because of Tuskegee's unique role as the USAAF's only air base for black airmen, it could graduate only limited numbers of students. Even so, on 26 May 1942, the 100th FS was activated at TAAF, pointing toward an all-black fighter group, and DeBow and Ross were duly assigned to the new unit. On 13 October, the 332nd FG was activated at Tuskegee, consisting of the 100th, 301st and 302nd FSs.

As pilots graduated, they joined an increasing number of personnel stationed at the base. The number of enlisted men trained to service the aircraft and support the units was also steadily increasing, with the 96th Service Group, 83rd Fighter Control Squadron and the 689th Signal Warning Company also sharing the base with the 332nd FG. By mid-1942, almost 220 officers and 3000 enlisted men were packed into TAAF. As a result, the 100th FS was despatched to Oscoda Army Airfield, in Michigan, where its arrival set a precedent – Oscoda was a white base, meaning that the 100th would be the first unit to de-segregate a USAAF facility, albeit temporarily.

Tuskegee would remain in operation throughout the war, graduating 1030 pilots by the time of its closure in 1949. Many of these men were assigned to the 477th Medium Bombardment Group, which was an

Training for the enlisted support personnel was carried out at Chanute Field before the men moved to Tuskegee. The number of enlisted men trained to service the aircraft and support the units was steadily increasing, with the 96th Service Group, 83rd Fighter Control Squadron and the 689th Signal Warning Company also sharing the base. By mid-1942, almost 220 officers and 3000 enlisted men were packed into TAAF (*Lt Col Harold C Hayes Collection*)

At the end of the training process, 2Lt Heber Houston gets his wings while Freddie Hutchins awaits his turn (*Lt Col Harold C Hayes Collection*)

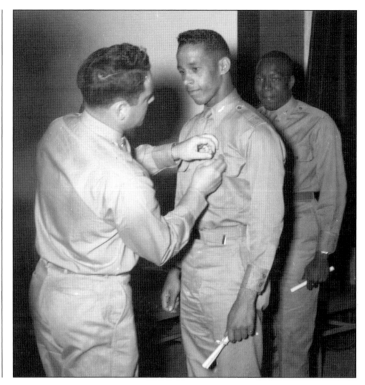

Cadets approaching the end of their training contemplate the site of their future service. Tuskegee was never fully able to meet the needs of the 332nd FG, the 477th Medium Bombardment Group and the call for liaison pilots in the Pacific, and this shortcoming forced black pilots to fly far more combat missions than their white counterparts (*Lt Col Harold C Hayes Collection*)

all-black B-25 unit that was so badly mishandled by the Army Air Force that it never made it into combat. A further 40 pilots from TAAF were sent to the Pacific, where they flew light aircraft as artillery spotters.

For the rest of the 'Tuskegee Airmen', their future was in fighters. In late 1942, the men of the 99th FS occupied themselves by conducting routine training flights, and speculating on why it was taking so long for them to be deployed to a combat theatre. For nine long months the unit languished at TAAF, and while the pilots were restless, this time 'later paid very great dividends', said Capt Benjamin Davis. During this period of combat inactivity 'we became a squadron. The 99th had a very great advantage from September 1942 until 15 April 1943, when it left Tuskegee. It was an active unit with no personal turbulence. The people got to know each other'.

While the squadron was awaiting orders, training took its inevitable toll. Richard C Davis was killed during a night flight in a P-40 on 30 January 1943, and two months later, on 24 March, Earl King was lost when his P-40 dived into Lake Martin, 20 miles north of the base. These pilots were replaced by 2Lts Sam M Bruce and James L McCullen.

On 1 April 1943, the 99th received its orders to head overseas. The squadron hurried to prepare for deployment, packing equipment and documents into boxes and personal equipment into trunks. By midnight, the men and their gear were loaded aboard a train for transport to Camp Shanks, New York, which would serve as their port of departure. On 15 April the squadron embarked on the troop ship *Mariposa* and slipped through the harbour fog. Through some coincidence, now-Lt Col Davis and his staff found themselves as the senior officers aboard the vessel, putting them in charge of the mixed-race complement of soldiers embarked in *Mariposa*. Lt Col Davis' father had been the first black man in history to command white officers and men of the US Army, and during the 99th's crossing, his son became the second.

'It was apparent, not only to me, but to the people in the 99th, that they held the future of blacks in the Army Air Corps in their hands', Davis said later. 'This was something that everyone in the 99th understood as early as the autumn of 1942 – that their performance would create the future environment for blacks'.

A 1942 line-up of red-cowled Vultee 'Vibrators' at Tuskegee. A cadre of civilian instructors supported the military instructor corps throughout the war (*Lt Col Harold C Hayes Collection*)

THE FIGHTING 99th

O n 24 April 1943, the *Mariposa* docked in Casablanca, Morocco. 'Spratmo' (gossip) aboard ship had suggested that, with the cold-weather clothing that the men had been issued, the 99th FS would be stationed in England. The sight of the brilliant blue skies and the dusty, refugee-filled streets quickly dispelled that notion. Lacking trucks, the men were forced to march with their equipment and gear for three miles in the oppressive mid-day sun to their bivouac area.

The one man not forced to march was Allen Lane, as he had broken his leg on his wedding day at the end of March. Lane, with his leg in a cast, bounced past his squadronmates aboard a jeep on the dusty road out of town shouting 'Okay, you dummies, on the double'! After setting up camp, Louis Purnell acquired a bottle of Coca-Cola – plentiful in port but rare in the field – to be saved as a prize for the unit's first aerial kill. It was secured in the squadron's safe.

A day later, the unit boarded an ancient train consisting of a locomotive, a coach and a dozen cattle cars for the 150-mile trip across French Morocco to the former Luftwaffe base at Oued Nja, near the town of Fez. The airfield was little more than a meadow ten miles north of the town of Meknes, at the base of the Atlas Mountains, with a large circle bulldozed nearby as a target for dive-bombing practice. Wrecked Bf 109s littered the airfield, and the squadron had to wait a week for its own aircraft to arrive – 27 Curtiss P-40Ls, Merlin-engined variants of the Warhawk that were lightened to improve performance. The P-40L lacked two of the P-40F's six machine guns, as well as about 100 lbs of armour around the oil cooler, engine and other vulnerable mechanical components.

The squadron used its time at Oued Nja to become familiar with the P-40L, and to study tactics. Pilots were assisted in both by the arrival of

The original cadre of pilots from the 99th FS pose for a photograph immediately prior to their deployment in April 1943. Sitting in the centre in the front row is Benjamin O Davis, and to his right is executive officer 'Spanky' Roberts. The latter would assume command of the unit from Davis on two occasions (*Lt Col Harold C Hayes Collection*)

three USAAF P-40 veterans of the desert campaign – Col Philip Corcoran and Majs Ralph Keyes and Robert Fackler. Corcoran, who was the real-life model for the character 'Flip Corkin' in the popular *Terry and the Pirates* comic strip, was 'particularly helpful to the 99th' remembered Charles Dryden. Living with the squadron for a week, he provided advice based on his own combat experiences.

'You P-40 pilots are the most courageous aviators in the war', Dryden recalled Corcoran saying. 'The Me 109 and the Fw 190 can outrun, out-climb and out-dive the P-40, so you'll have to stay and fight! But there's one thing you can do – the P-40 can out-turn every fighter the Germans have, except one built by the Italians, the Macchi 202, and there aren't many of those in the theatre. So if you get jumped, get into a tight turn, reef it in as tight as you can without stalling and just wait him out. If he tries to stay with you, you'll eventually end up on his tail'. Corcoran also flew with the squadron and tutored them on dive-bombing – a skill that would prove useful in the coming months.

On one training flight, 'Bud' Clark's landing gear failed to lower properly, and, after burning off excess fuel, he coolly set the P-40L down on its belly with minimal damage. His actions earned him the title of 'Yank of the Month' from the Army's *Yank* newspaper! Another P-40L was saved by Leon Roberts after he clipped a wire, lopping off the top of the rudder and vertical stabiliser. Roberts nursed the damaged Warhawk back to Oued Nja and put it down safely.

At the end of May 1943, with its training deemed complete, the squadron moved 1000 miles east to Fardjouna, on Tunisia's Cap Bon Peninsula. 'The flying out of Cap Bon could be quite hazardous in that we flew off a dirt strip', Benjamin Davis recalled. 'We would take-off in a 12-aeroplane formation. Although we never had a collision, it was a hairy operation, especially if you had to get back into the field soon after take-off in case of an emergency – if there was no cross-wind to blow the dust away, the strip would be totally obscured'.

Fardjouna also had plenty of German-made diversions for the pilots. Bernard 'Jim' Knighten, known to his fellow pilots as 'the Eel', got an abandoned kubelwagen working, and Gene Carter found a German motorcycle among the piles of destroyed German aircraft littering the field.

33rd FG

The squadron was attached to the 33rd FG under the command of Col William 'Spike' Momyer. The group had made an inauspicious start to combat operations at Fardjouna, for when Momyer led its 75 P-40s into the base for the first time, 21 of them crashed on landing. Recovering from this early setback, the 33rd had enjoyed great success on its first day in combat from its new base in January 1943, knocking down eight aeroplanes. However, it had since been so badly mauled in subsequent battles that it had to stand down to re-equip. The 99th FS was assigned in an effort to make good those losses.

Momyer made his antipathy for the squadron known immediately. When Davis and 'Spanky' Roberts reported, Momyer did not return their salutes. On 3 June he scheduled a briefing, then moved the time up by an hour without telling the 99th, so the men arrived late. His efforts to

Willie Fuller reads a letter from home while sitting on the wing of his Warhawk *RUTHEA*. Fuller would complete 70 missions before the end of his tour (*Herman Lawson via the National Museum of the USAF*)

embarrass the squadron badly affected its reputation, and only later would the full extent of Momyer's damage be understood.

Twenty-four hours prior to the infamous late briefing, the 99th FS had flown its first combat sorties when William Campbell and Clarence Jamison flew as wingmen to other 33rd FG fighters on an offensive sweep, followed several hours later by a second group operation that involved James Wiley and Charlie Hall. They bombed and strafed the German-held airfield on the island of Pantelleria, 47 miles east of Cap Bon, during the course of both missions. Wiley flew as wingman to Momyer, his P-40L (like all the others involved) carrying 500-lb bombs. All four 99th FS pilots dived and dropped their ordnance upon cues given to them by their flight leaders. The next day, the four pilots that had been wingmen on the 2nd led a second bombing strike against the same target.

Attacks on Axis forces on Pantelleria continued, with the 99th rotating its pilots through the missions to give them combat experience. On 4 June Charles Dryden got his chance, his entry into combat having been delayed when wingman Willie Ashley's P-40L experienced a rough-running engine during the squadron's flight from Oued Nja. Dryden and Ashley had been forced to land at the depot at Oujda, where new P-40s were being assembled.

Although the depot personnel did not have time to repair the engine problem, they were willing to give the pilots new P-40Ls to replace the 'old' ones! The next morning, Dryden's original P-40L, *A TRAIN*, was left behind and replaced by *A TRAIN II*.

On 4 June he found himself over Pantelleria with a 500-lb bomb strapped to the belly of his fighter. 'Following my leader in a dive, I saw hundreds of red tracers streaking past my cockpit', Dryden remembered. 'Concentrating on hitting the target, I didn't have time to get scared. It

Crewmen carry out maintenance on a P-40L in the late afternoon sun at Fardjouna during the 99th FS's campaign against Sicily (*National Museum of the USAF*)

wasn't until I pulled up from the bomb run that the thought crossed my mind that they were trying to kill me!'

The pilots of the 99th failed to encounter any opposition in the air until 9 June, when six P-40Ls piloted by Dryden, Ashley, Sidney Brooks, Lee Rayford, Leon Roberts and Spann Watson provided top cover for a dozen A-20 Havocs attacking Pantelleria. The flight spotted four unidentified aeroplanes at 'five o'clock high', and several minutes later they dived on the formation. Identifying them as Bf 109s, the P-40L pilots turned into the German fighters and a melee ensued that thoroughly tested the flying skills of the men from the 99th FS.

Rayford found two Bf 109s on his tail, and seconds later their bullets stitched across his right wing. However, Spann Watson opened fire on the Germans from long range and convinced them to abandon their attack. Meanwhile, Ashley's excited turn into the enemy induced his P-40L to start spinning uncontrollably. He quickly lost several thousand feet in height directly over Pantelleria.

Corcoran had urged the men never to split up, and with this in mind, Ashley was eager to join up with the only other aeroplane he could see nearby. However, he soon realised that this fighter was in fact an Fw 190! Ashley opened fire and the Focke-Wulf began to smoke, but persistent ground fire forced the 99th FS pilot to abandon his chase and kept him from confirming that his adversary had indeed crashed.

Meanwhile, Dryden had spotted a formation of 12 Ju 88s above him, and he immediately set off after them. Unfortunately, the unit's P-40Ls were set up for low-level operations, and therefore lacked the essential oxygen system that the pilot needed when operating at altitudes in excess of 15,000 ft. Dryden, having climbed to 16,000 ft, and still out of range of the German bombers, passed out. He came to after his aeroplane had stalled into a shallow dive and descended several thousand feet.

Willie Ashley smiles as he boards his Warhawk. Ashley damaged an Fw 190 on 9 June 1943, and although the German fighter was last seen trailing smoke, no witnesses saw it crash, thus depriving the pilot of the squadron's first kill (*Lt Col Harold C Hayes Collection*)

All six pilots returned safely from the mission, elated at having survived their first brush with their German counterparts. However, their eagerness for a fight would be characterised as 'panicky' and 'undisciplined' by Momyer in his official report on the engagement to the Army Air Force. He would continue to deliberately minimise and mis-characterise the squadron's achievements in his communiqués to XII Fighter Command HQ throughout his tenure as CO of the 33rd FG.

BASE MOVE

On 11 June 1943, after being pounded by the Allies' Mediterranean air forces, Pantelleria surrendered, thus becoming the first territory ever captured purely by the use of air power alone. The 33rd FG moved to El Haouaria a short while later, and the group set its sights on Sicily – the Allies' next major target. Following a short break from the action, on 2 July the squadron was assigned to escort 16 B-25s sent to bomb a

German airfield in the Castelveltrano area of Sicily as part of a larger mission that involved 72 fighters and about the same number of Mitchells, Havocs and Marauders.

The lead Mitchell missed the initial point for its run in to the target, forcing the remaining 15 bombers to circle directly overhead the target. Meanwhile, the P-40L pilots could see plumes of dust on the airfield below as German fighters hastily scrambled to meet them. The B-25s dropped their bombs, then started a gentle descending left turn to head back to their bases in Africa.

At that point, having managed to climb above the escorts, the German fighters took full advantage of their superior altitude and made a slashing attack on the 99th FS. The P-40Ls of Sherman White and James McCullen simply disappeared as a result of this pass, having undoubtedly fallen victim to defending fighters. In the blink of an eye, these men had become the first members of the squadron to die in action.

As the bombers continued to make their turn, Charlie 'Seabuster' Hall spotted a pair of Fw 190s stalking them. Positioning himself behind the trailing fighter, he fired off a long burst that struck the Focke-Wulf. The latter machine then lurched from a gentle left turn into an abrupt dive, and Hall followed his victim down until he saw it hit the ground in a 'big cloud of dust'. Moments after losing two pilots to the German fighters, the 99th had scored its first aerial victory. At about the same time that Hall secured the squadron's premier victory, 'Ghost' Lawson also fired at an Fw 190 and claimed it as probably destroyed – he damaged a Bf 109 moments later.

Meanwhile, two Bf 109s had made a head-on pass at the sections led by Dryden and 'Bill' Campbell. Dryden called the break, but an apparent radio malfunction kept Campbell from hearing him, so the former threw his P-40L into a turn and fired at the Germans as they climbed away for another attack. Within seconds Dryden was alone, and he searched the sky for a friendly fighter. Eventually, he spotted a P-40L about 500 ft below him, flying straight and level.

As he descended to join up, Dryden observed two Bf 109s stalking the American fighter, and he latched onto their tails. He opened fire and damaged the trailing Messerschmitt, but a spurt of tracer flying past Dryden's cockpit snapped his head around. Close behind him was a third enemy fighter. Following Corcoran's directives, Dryden hauled *A TRAIN II* into a tight turn, but instead of getting onto the enemy fighter's tail, the P-40 pilot found that his foe was staying with him in the turn and drawing a bead on him!

'The first time around, I saw the top of his canopy', said Dryden. 'The next time around, I saw his nose, and the next time around I saw his belly. At that point I realised it was a Macchi 202!'

Charlie 'Seabuster' Hall poses in the cockpit of his P-40L Warhawk. On 2 July 1943, Hall became the first member of the 99th FS to score a kill when he downed an Fw 190 over Castelveltrano. Walter 'Ghost' Lawson claimed a probable and damaged a second fighter, but the day was bittersweet, for Sherman White and James McCullen failed to return – probably victims of a mid-air collision (*National Museum of the USAF*)

Mechanics troubleshoot a war-weary P-40L's tired Merlin engine in late 1943. This variant of the Warhawk was lightened by the omission of two machine guns and almost 200 lbs of armour (*National Museum of the USAF*)

Transfixed, Dryden watched as the Macchi C.202's wing-mounted 20 mm cannon belched what he thought looked like 'dirty grey cotton balls' at his aeroplane. One shell blew a chunk out of his left wing, and Dryden desperately called for help. 'Jim' Knighten heard him and pulled up from the bombers he was escorting and settled into a tight diving turn that placed him behind the Macchi. A burst from Knighten's guns sent the Italian fighter fleeing.

Dryden waved a thank you, and he and Knighten turned back in the direction of North Africa, only to be bounced by two more Bf 109s that attacked from below. The Americans and Germans 'scissored' back and forth for about ten minutes, with neither side able to gain an advantage. At one point, Dryden and Knighten thought that they had lost their pursuers, so they dived for the deck, only to spot the two Bf 109s duplicating their manoeuvre which in turn led them to resume the turning duel. Eventually, even the lone C.202 rejoined the fight, but soon the enemy fighters realised that they were being drawn into Allied territory, and they sped north towards Sicily.

Arriving back at Fardjouna, Hall performed a victory roll, and Louis Purnell travelled 15 miles to secure a block of ice to cool the prized bottle of Coca-Cola, which Hall enjoyed in the shade of a grove of olive trees.

Once the Allies had established a beachhead on Sicily on 10 July, the squadron flew patrols from Gela to Licata to dissuade the Luftwaffe from harassing the invasion fleet. On the 11th, Dick Bolling's fighter was hit by flak and he bailed out over the Mediterranean. Spending the night

23

'Jim' Knighten, seen here taxiing his P-40L *EEL II*, came to the rescue of Charles Dryden after the latter's fighter had been holed by a Macchi C.202 on 2 July 1943. Out of the cockpit, Knighten's ability to acquire languages seemingly overnight, and his sense of humour, made him a favourite among the 99th (*National Air and Space Museum*)

bobbing about in his rubber life raft, he was rescued and returned to the squadron on 12 July. Eight days later, the 99th FS relocated to Licata, with its ground echelon and equipment being crammed into 30 C-47s which were in turn escorted by the units own P-40Ls.

Heartened by the actions of 2 July, the 99th FS had no way of knowing that it would not spot another enemy fighter for six months. Instead of

Charlie Hall displays his trophy – a bottle of Coca-Cola – for downing the 99th's first kill (*Elmer Jones via National Air and Space Museum*)

99th FS Warhawks taxi to the
runway at Licata in mid-July 1943.
The group would fly from this
Sicilian base until October, when it
moved to Foggia, on mainland Italy
(*National Air and Space Museum*)

flying bomber escort missions, pilots would be assigned 'dangerous and dirty' ground support sorties for the rest of 1943.

Because of the segregated nature of the squadron, the 99th's pilots flew more missions – as many as six per day – than their white counterparts. TAAF simply could not graduate pilots quickly enough to offset attrition, which meant that the squadron's first replacements did not arrive until 23 July, when Howard Baugh, John Gibson, Ed Toppins and John Morgan landed in North Africa. The pilots' arrival had been further delayed by a mix up in military transportation that left them stranded in Brazil for three weeks!

Several days later Robert Diez, Elwood 'Woody' Driver, Herman 'Ace' Lawson, Clinton 'Beau' Mills and Henry 'Herky' Perry also joined the squadron.

Dive-bombing and ground support missions continued unabated until 11 August, when a flying accident claimed another pilot. Whilst performing a diving attack on a target, Graham Mitchell developed engine trouble and veered into the path of Sam 'Lizard' Bruce's fighter. Bruce pulled up sharply, and while he avoided a collision, his propeller sliced off the tail of Mitchell's P-40L. The latter pilot was killed, but Bruce parachuted to safety.

FIGHTING TO SURVIVE

On 2 September Lt Col Davis was recalled to the USA to take command of the 332nd FG, but instead of going directly to Selfridge Field, he first went to the Pentagon.

The efforts of Momyer and others in the Army Air Force to have the 99th sent back to the USA or to some out-of-the-way theatre had led to an article in *Time* magazine entitled 'Experiment Proved?' It stated that the 99th might be disbanded, based on a report from Momyer claiming that the group did not fight as a team, broke formation when attacked, opted for undefended targets instead of defended briefed targets, avoided bad weather and, in general, performed poorly. 'It is my opinion that they are not of the fighting calibre of any squadron in this group', Momyer wrote in his official report. 'They have failed to display the aggressiveness and daring for combat that are necessary for a first class fighting organisation. It may be expected that we will get less work and less operational time out of the 99th FS than any squadron in this group'.

Lt Col Davis' appearance before a Congressional committee evaluating the 99th FS's performance proved critical to the future success of the 332nd FG. His testimony contradicted the reports from 'Spike' Momyer, and inspired a command-level study of all Twelfth Air Force Warhawk squadrons that revealed the capabilities of the 99th both quantifiably and irrefutably (*Lt Col Harold C Hayes Collection*)

Momyer's superior, Brig Gen Edwin House, agreed, and the report was endorsed by Maj Gen John Cannon, deputy commanding general of the Allied Tactical Air Force for the Sicilian campaign. Lt Gen Carl 'Tooey' Spaatz, deputy commander of the Mediterranean Allied Air Forces, added his opinion that the 99th be reassigned to coastal patrol duty in a location such as the Panama Canal Zone.

'I was absolutely infuriated', said Davis. He was called to testify before a Congressional committee evaluating the squadron's performance, and the viability of the training of black airmen. 'I'm sure that all the aces were held by the Army Air Force', Davis explained, 'especially with the correspondence going up through channels the way it did, and the statement by Gen House that a Negro didn't possess the physical qualifications that would make him a good fighter pilot'.

Davis, accustomed to remaining composed in the face of overt racism, told the committee that the men of the squadron were no different from any other Americans at war in other USAAF squadrons, and their performance paralleled that of other units. 'I recall saying something to the effect that overseas, the reception given to black people on the ground was much more pleasant and more favourable than the reception given to black people on the ground here in the United States. I also stressed the determination of the members of the 99th to demonstrate their abilities and set the stage for the oncoming combat units that were still training in the states'.

Davis explained that the 99th had received only 26 pilots since its formation, compared to 30-35 sent to most other fighter squadrons in the same period. This meant that his pilots flew as many as six sorties per day. Furthermore, the ground attack missions handed down to the squadron meant that it was less likely to encounter enemy aircraft, accounting for its low air-to-air score.

Having heard Davis' argument, 'Hap' Arnold said that he would take no action until a study of the performance of all P-40 units in the theatre could be completed. Even so, Arnold remained unconvinced that black aviators could perform well in forward combat zones, and he advocated their relocation to a rear defence area. The committee's report, slated to be delivered to President Roosevelt, was revised and edited by Col Emmett O'Donnell.

Bucking the tendencies of his superior officers, O'Donnell included a cover memo which 'urgently recommended that this entire subject be reconsidered'. He pointed out the absurdity of discrimination during wartime, and he observed that one to four squadrons were but a drop in the overall war effort. Furthermore, 'I feel that such a proposal (to disband the 99th) to the President at this time would definitely not be appreciated by him', O'Donnell wrote. 'He would probably interpret it as indicating a serious lack of understanding of the broad problems facing the country'. Roosevelt never received the report.

When the results of Arnold's study eventually made it to the Pentagon, it proved that the 99th FS was as good as, or better than, other Warhawk units in the Mediterranean. 'If that G-3 evaluation had not been made, God knows what would have happened', Davis recalled.

He also noted that the report had a secondary effect. 'It sent us to the Fifteenth Air Force, and took us out of the nasty, dirty close air support business, and put us into a sort of glamour business – escorting bombers. Sometimes things turn out for the best, and that's exactly what happened'.

In Davis' absence, 'Spanky' Roberts assumed command of the 99th, with Lemuel Custis as operations officer. The same day that Davis departed for the USA, advance elements of the 99th moved from Licata to the Italian mainland following the Allied landings at Salerno.

Upon arriving at their assigned base, the advance party found not a prepared airfield but an active battleground, and they soon came under fire. Their base was still in German hands following a counter-attack against the British Army's X Corps, and a second potential field had been repeatedly bombed and strafed by the Luftwaffe. Five days later X Corps repulsed the German attack, and work began on setting up the new field.

The rest of the squadron moved 62 miles from Licata to Termini (a town on the northern coast of Sicily), followed two weeks later by another base change to Barcelona, 70 miles to the east.

Sydney Brooks, clad in extremely non-traditional flight garb, poses in front on his P-40F *"EL CID"/JOYCE* – this aircraft was one of only a handful of F-models issued to the 99th FS. Brooks, a graduate of the second class from TAAF, died 24 hours after crash-landing Charles Dryden's *A TRAIN II* on 18 August 1943 (*National Air and Space Museum*)

On 26 September orders reached the squadron instructing Dryden, Rayford, Purnell, 'Peepsight' Smith and 'Ghost' Lawson to return home so that they could impart their combat knowledge to students at TAAF. Their moment of happiness literally went up in smoke though when Sidney Brooks crashed on take-off in Dryden's *A TRAIN II*. Brooks' own fighter, *El Cid*, had had a rough-running engine when he started it up, so in an effort to take-off with the rest of the unit, he jumped into Dryden's fighter.

As Brooks climbed away from the runway, witnesses heard his engine start to splutter. Brooks turned back and executed a neat wheels-up landing, but he failed to drop his belly tank, which sheared off on contact with the ground, then bounced after the Warhawk and exploded against it. Brooks leapt from the cockpit, his flight suit smouldering. As a precaution, he was taken to a British field hospital, and he seemed well enough to make efforts to check himself out that night. However, when his squadronmates came to visit him the next morning, Sidney Brooks was dead, a victim of secondary shock and smoke inhalation.

INTO ITALY

Such was the resistance put up by the Germans at Salerno that the advanced echelon and the rest of the 99th FS did not finally reunite until 17 October at Foggia No 3 airfield. This move coincided with the squadron also receiving a new assignment which saw it leave Momyer's 33rd FG for the 79th FG, led by Col Earl Bates. The latter was thankfully bereft of the biases that had affected the way Momyer dealt with the 99th, and the squadron's combat experience changed considerably.

An indication of Bates' attitude towards the squadron can be gained from the fact that the group's war diaries never once mention the skin colour of the men of the 99th FG. He made sure that the 99th routinely flew missions alongside his other squadrons, and at times had black pilots leading mixed formations that included aircraft from other units in the group.

Combat operations resumed on 20 October, when the 99th bombed and strafed shipping targets in the Isernia-Capionne area and hunted for road traffic northwest of Sangro. Two days later the squadron attacked German ammunition dumps in a mission in which two P-40Ls were damaged by flak. Continual beach patrol and armed reconnaissance missions kept the squadron busy, but the Luftwaffe was notable by its absence.

Early November brought a spate of harsh weather, making flying dangerous and life on the ground miserable – the airmen were not immune from the famous Italian mud. Despite the trying conditions, the 99th averaged 48 sorties per day in support of the British crossing of the river Sangro later in the month, and on 22 November James Wiley became the first member of the squadron to completed 50 missions.

Three days prior to Wiley reaching his 'half century', the 79th FG had begun a move to Madna, which was a coastal airstrip near Termoli. The pace of operations increased following the base swap, and on 30 November alone, the squadron flew nine missions.

During the first week in December, newcomer 2Lt Alva Temple clipped a fence in his P-40L at the end of the still-unfamiliar Madna

Groundcrewmen fuel a P-40 Warhawk nicknamed *SWELL* at Madna, in Italy, on 30 December 1943. The perforated steel plating runway seen here was commonplace at the group's various Italian airfields (*National Museum of the USAF*)

field on take-off, damaging the Warhawk's landing gear. Instead of turning back, he completed the mission with one wheel partially retracted, then made a crash-landing at Madna that ripped the left wing off his P-40L, *Nona II*.

Despite now flying in a group that genuinely appreciated the 99th FS's efforts in combat, morale was at a low ebb in December 1943 due to a combination of poor weather, dangerous missions made worse by a marginal airfield from which to operate and increasingly combat weary aircraft. It sank even lower on 2 January 1944 when John Morgan was killed. Morgan's P-40 landed down-wind, and he was unable to stop the fighter before it slammed into a ditch at the end of the runway. The rain, mud, lack of aerial opposition and gradual understanding that enemies within the USAAF were even more relentless than the Germans in trying to destroy the squadron weighed heavily on the 99th.

On 15 January Lt William Griffin's Warhawk was shot down over enemy territory, and he remained a prisoner of war until May 1945. The next day, the 99th moved from the east coast of the Italian 'boot' to Capodichino, near Naples on the west coast, so as to be closer to the coming amphibious assault on Anzio. The latter offensive began in the early hours of 22 January, and as the invasion bogged down, the Luftwaffe began to reappear. The opportunity to engage German aircraft once again proved to be a turning point in the 99th FS's war.

AERIAL COMBAT AGAIN

At about 0830 hrs on the morning of 27 January, a formation of 16 Warhawks led by Lt Clarence Jamison spotted 15 Fw 190s dive-bombing shipping off St Peter's Beach and dived into the enemy formation. All through the swirling melee which ensued, aircraft identification proved very simple according to some 99th FS pilots because the German fighters were about 80 mph faster than their P-40Ls!

As the German *Jabos* reacted by diving for the deck, eager to escape the beachhead, Jamison and Ashley executed a 'split-S' and found themselves directly above the German flight leader and his wingman. Jamison opened fire and 'hits were registered on the right wing, and chunks flew off', but his four 0.50-cal machine guns then jammed and he was only given credit for an aircraft damaged. Ashley stuck to his quarry and chased him at deck level to within a few miles of Rome, getting so close that he could see the pilot before he opened fire. Bullets peppered the Fw 190 and it burst into flames.

Howard Baugh and wingman Clarence Allen dropped behind another fleeing Fw 190, their fire forcing the fighter-bomber to hit the ground at a shallow angle and crash, giving them each a half-kill. Robert Diez, spotting an unsuspecting Fw 190 flying on a parallel course to him at about 750 ft to his left, dropped in behind the Focke-Wulf and opened fire. The Fw 190's cowling flew off and the aeroplane dived into a yard near a farmhouse. Ed Toppins latched himself onto the tail of yet another Fw 190 and fired a short burst. The aeroplane bobbed up and then dropped its nose and exploded when it hit the ground.

One Fw 190 pilot who had had enough space between his machine and Leon Roberts' P-40L to pull away and escape instead chose to stay and fight. In a turning engagement that lasted several minutes, Roberts patiently fired and corrected over the course of a sequence of turns before finally hitting the German aircraft, which flipped over onto its back and plummeted to earth.

'Herky' Perry dived on a Focke-Wulf just as it levelled out of a dive and 'raked the enemy ship from head to tail at about 300 yards. The aeroplane seemed to flutter, then fell off on the wing and headed for the ground'.

One of the 99th FS's first replacements was Howard Baugh, seen here standing ramrod straight in a cadet photograph. Baugh and Clarence Allen combined to destroy an Fw 190 on 27 January, shooting it up as it was attempting to escape at low altitude (*Lt Col Harold C Hayes Collection*)

Robert W Diez went from being a track star at the University of Oregon to one of the 99th's first replacement pilots. On 28 January 1944, Diez shot an Fw 190 off the tail of his wingman to tally his second kill (*Western Aerospace Museum*)

Men of the 99th FS re-enact one of
the 13 kills scored on 27-28 January
1944 in front of a Warhawk that
still appears to being wearing an
Operation *Torch*-style surround to its
national marking. The victories over
Anzio came after months without
air-to-air action, and provided a
morale boost to both the squadron
and pilots in the 332nd FG, who
learned of the successes aboard
a troop ship bound for Italy
(*National Museum of the USAF*)

Perry's prey was recorded as damaged. Jack Rogers and 'Woody' Driver
cut off another Rome-bound Fw 190 and holed it with gunfire, losing
sight of the fighter as it was smoking and in a steep dive at a height of just
50 ft. They were given a share in the probable kill.

The day was not yet done, however, for that afternoon Lemuel Custis
led another patrol over Anzio, and inland from the beach he stumbled
upon a mixed formation of Fw 190s and Bf 109s. The pilots of these
aeroplanes had more fight in them than the ones encountered that
morning, and almost immediately an Fw 190 got on the tail of Lt Erwin
Lawrence's P-40L. Lt Wilson 'Sloppy' Eagleson spotted Lawrence's
evasive manoeuvring and cut across the path of the two aircraft, snapping

Wilson Eagleson smiles from the
cockpit of his well-worn Warhawk,
surrounded by Lemuel Custis,
Willie Ashley and Charlie Hall.
Eagleson returned to Italy for a
second tour in Mustangs in 1944
(*Bernard Proctor via the National
Museum of the USAF*)

off a 90-degree deflection shot at the Focke-Wulf, which burst into flames and hit the ground.

Lawrence, in turn, found himself set up for a deflection shot on another Fw 190, and Eagleson subsequently reported seeing his squadronmate's Fw 190 'roll over and dive for the ground, smoking excessively'. Lawrence was credited with a probable.

Custis, meanwhile, spotted an Fw 190 on the deck trying to escape. After chasing it to within seven miles of Rome, he 'let loose a burst of fire, and saw tracers hit his fuselage and the aeroplane crash'. Charles Bailey caught another retreating Fw 190 with an outstanding 45-degree deflection shot, causing the pilot to bail out of his stricken machine.

The German fighters extracted some measure of revenge, however, with Allen Lane finding himself the focus of at least four Fw 190s, which riddled his P-40L and forced him to bail out. Sam Bruce was last seen chasing a pair of Fw 190s, but apparently he was set upon by more German fighters and forced to abandon his fighter. Although his parachute deployed, Bruce was found to be dead when he hit the ground.

Rumours quickly circulated about Bruce's cause of death, some stating that he had been deliberately killed by a South African Air Force Spitfire pilot who machine gunned him in his 'chute because he was black, while others suggested it was more likely that he was mortally wounded by flak or by fire from the enemy aircraft that downed him.

The next day, Charlie Hall's flight spotted a flight of Bf 109s and Fw 190s at 4000 ft approaching Anzio from the north. The Warhawk pilots had a 1000-ft altitude advantage, and they dived on the German fighters, which again turned away. 'Six enemy aeroplanes came down in a string. We intercepted them at 3000 ft and followed them on the deck', Hall told correspondent Art Carter. He closed in to 300 yards before he began firing on one of the Bf 109s. 'I gave it two bursts of fire. It flamed and crashed to the ground'. Hall then wheeled the P-40L around 'and chased an Fw 190 towards Rome', moving to within 200 yards of his target before opening fire.

Meanwhile, C C 'Curtis' Robinson was diving and firing at another German aeroplane when a 'brown blur' – Hall's Warhawk – flashed in front of him. Somehow Robinson managed not to hit his flight leader, but he saw Hall 'giving it short bursts' until the Fw 190 snapped into a spin and hit the ground.

Lewis Smith had also spotted a target soon after the flight had intercepted the German fighters. 'The sky was full of aeroplanes, but I picked out an Fw 190 and chased him to the outskirts of Rome, firing all the way', he told Carter. When he was in position to fire a 50-degree deflection shot, Smith depressed the trigger. 'The (enemy) aircraft veered out of control about 20 ft above the ground and burst into flames', Smith reported. 'It burned and smoked profusely, and I knew I had got him'.

Robert Diez' wingman found an Fw 190 on his tail, so he dragged it across the path of his leader's machine by breaking in front of him. Diez coolly despatched his second enemy fighter in two days. 'A portion of the ship's cowling flew off and it went into a steep dive at about 750 ft', Diez reported.

Two days of fighting had brought 13 confirmed kills, which dispelled any doubts about the inability of black pilots to perform in aerial combat.

'We've been looking forward to this happening, but this is the first time in five months that we have encountered enemy opposition in the air', 'Spanky' Roberts told Carter. 'We poured hell into them'.

INVASION PROTECTION

The resurgence of the Luftwaffe coincided with the difficulties the Allies were having on the ground at Anzio. The squadron's critical ground support responsibilities were supplemented with an increasing number of patrols designed to keep German aircraft from strafing and bombing the troops.

On 5 February, a patrol over the beachhead was headed west at about 6000 ft when it spotted at least ten Fw 190s diving towards the beach from a height of 16,000 ft, before flattening out on the deck. The P-40s quickly turned into the German aircraft, and Elwood Driver made a diving left turn and pulled up about 300 yards behind an Fw 190. He began firing 'and continued to fire in long bursts, even though my target was pulling

SSgt McGary L Edwards of Elkins, West Virginia, was captured on film by an Army Air Force photographer while hard at work on a P-40L at Capodichino on 23 March 1944. The intensity of the Anzio campaign shows in the condition of the Warhawk's propeller – sand has abraded all the paint from the leading edges (*National Museum of the USAF*)

away', he reported. 'My tracers straddled the cockpit and a sheet of flames burst from the right side. I last saw the aeroplane burning and headed towards Rome at a height of just 50 ft above the ground'.

At the same time, Clarence Jamison and George McCrumby were tangling with six Fw 190s when the latter pilot's P-40L was struck by anti-aircraft fire. 'Something hit underneath my ship', McCrumby told Carter. 'Then another burst cracked the side of my cockpit, plunging the aeroplane into a dive at 4000 ft. I tried to pull out but had no control. The elevators had been knocked out. I had no alternative but to jump'.

After sliding the canopy back, McCrumby tried to clamber out the left side of the P-40L, but was thrown back in his seat by the slipstream. 'Then I tried the right side and got half way out when again the slipstream threw me against the fuselage', he said. 'I struggled until all but my right foot was free and dangled from the diving aeroplane until the wind turned the ship around at about 1000 ft and shook me loose. I reached for the rip cord six times before finding it, but my parachute opened immediately, landing me safely in a cow pasture.'

Meanwhile, Jamison's aeroplane had been riddled by fire from one of the six Fw 190s he and McCrumby had gone after, and whilst trying to escape his Merlin engine overheated and seized up. He crash-landed the Warhawk in a field near the frontline and was rescued by US Army Rangers.

Forty-eight hours later, two more Fw 190s were downed, with Leonard Jackson and Clinton Mills each receiving credit for a kill. But the Germans had learned from their experiences with the nimble P-40Ls, opting now to rely on their superior speed in order to avoid engagements. Several of the patrols in February encountered German fighters, but these simply pulled away from Warhawks in the subsequent tail chase that ensued.

When Clarence Allen was shot down north of Rome in the late afternoon of March 1944, he took shelter in a cave, where he slept overnight. The next morning, Allen discovered he was camping in the middle of a German bivouac area! He lay low until the Germans moved on, then evaded capture and returned to the 99th (*Lt Col Harold C Hayes Collection*)

Still, the dive-bombing skills that the squadron had honed over the past eight months made them valuable assets, and they were recognised as such by the Luftwaffe, which bombed Capodichino for 30 minutes on the night of 14 March. The next day, Mt Vesuvius erupted, spewing ash and rock that inflicted more damage on the Allied air forces in Italy than the Luftwaffe could have ever hoped to have done. Luckily, the 99th FS was little affected by either event.

On 19 March the squadron was tasked with knocking out the 'Anzio Express' rail gun that was causing problems by shelling the beaches and airfields. Eight P-40s were sent out to find tunnel openings in which the gun might be hidden, and after dropping four bombs on a suspect tunnel, pilots also strafed the target. One P-40 was damaged by flak, but the 'Express' was permanently silenced.

The squadron also played a part in Operation *Strangle*, which saw Allied aircraft interdicting German transport trains linking the Po Valley and troops holding up the advance from Anzio. During one of these missions, Clarence Allen was shot down north of Rome, and he hid out overnight in a cave. The following morning he discovered that he had been hiding in the middle of a German bivouac area! Eventually, once the German troops had moved out, Allen evaded capture and returned to the 99th FS.

Later in the month, after a successful dive-bombing mission against road traffic, Howard Baugh and Lewis 'Smirkin'' Smith spotted a convoy of German trucks and dropped down to strafe it, but they made the mistake of flying parallel to the road, instead of at an angle. Smith's aircraft was hit, and Baugh saw him bail out. Smith was not as lucky as Allen – captured almost immediately, he would spend the next 14 months as a prisoner of war.

Despite the lack of recent aerial opposition, the squadron's tally during the Anzio campaign stood at 17, while the total for the three regular squadrons in the 79th FG was 32 (15 for the 85th, two for the 86th and 15 for the 87th). Contrary to the article it published in September 1943, *Time* magazine reported, 'The Air Force regards its experiment proven'.

On 2 April the 99th FS moved to Cercola airfield, where it was attached to the 324th FG, commanded by Col Leonard Lydon. Other changes included the departure of CO Maj 'Spanky' Roberts back to the USA, his place being taken by Capt Erwin Lawrence.

The squadron participated in the battle for Monte Cassino in May, pounding German positions during the push for Rome. By the time Rome fell on 4 June, the 99th had flown 500 missions and 3277 sorties. Following a brief stay at Ciampo airfield, and assignment to the 86th FG, the squadron moved to Ramitelli airfield on 28 June, where it joined the three squadrons of the 332nd FG.

Lt Theodore 'Ted' Wilson collects his parachute after bailing out on 4 May 1944 over Cercola. Wilson's Warhawk had been disabled by flak during a ground attack mission, but he was able to nurse the crippled aeroplane home before 'hitting the silk' (*Western Aerospace Museum*)

AIRACOBRAS AND THUNDERBOLTS

On 22 December 1943, a train left Oscoda Field, Michigan, bound for Fort Patrick Henry, Virginia, carrying the men of the 100th, 301st and 302nd FSs. Having trained at Tuskegee and other bases in the USA, the group was now under the command of Lt Col Benjamin O Davis. After his combat experiences with the 99th FS, the group was initially a disappointment. He described them as a 'gaggle' of pilots who had been 'moved around from pillar to post. They'd been to school here and there, but they had not flown enough as a unit'.

While the 99th had had nine months to train, the 100th, 301st and 302nd had not enjoyed such a lengthy work up. Davis blamed the units' early problems on the lack of a cadre of trained pilots and groundcrew who could have imparted their experience and attitudes on the men. They also suffered from a shortage of proper fighter trainers – the worn-out P-40Cs they had flown at Oscoda had directly led to the deaths of two 2Lts Wilmeth Sadat-Singh and Jerome Edwards.

Initially under the command of Lt Col Samuel Westbrook, the group was turned over to Col Robert Selway in June 1943, who did his job efficiently. He would subsequently impose segregationist policies on the 477th Medium Bombardment Group that effectively prevented it from succeeding. Much to the joy of the men, Selway was replaced by Lt Col Davis in October 1943, and just before Christmas the group shipped out.

The 332nd's first battle came in Virginia, where the local motion picture theatre featured a roped-off area for 'coloured' troops. The angered men of the group were ordered confined to quarters by Davis, who then warned the base commander that he would not assume

This panoramic view of the field at Montecorvino sums up the operational lot of the 332nd FG during its harbour patrol era – four war-weary P-39s, many tents and a lot of mud (*National Museum of the USAF*)

responsibility for the actions of his men if theatre segregation was not ended. The ropes came down, but tensions remained high until the group boarded a convoy of troopships on 2 January 1944. During the trip, the group's spirits were lifted by news of the 99th's successes over the Anzio beachhead.

The 332nd's convoy arrived in the Italian port of Taranto 32 days later. 'It was a terrible sight because of the bombings', said Samuel Curtis. 'Rusting ships were overturned in the harbour. Most of the Italian structures were built out of stone and masonry, and they had been bombed by the Americans first and then, of course, when the Allies took it, the Germans bombed the port too. There was white dusty powder all over everything, and an unpleasant smell that went along with the sights. As the ships pulled up in the dock, we saw these people, these human beings in ragged clothes, with babies. They were going around begging and looking into garbage cans for food. It was a very disturbing sight'.

The 100th FS had set up shop in Montecorvino by 5 February, and the rumours that they would be equipped with the P-38 or the new P-63 Kingcobra were soon dispelled, as waiting for them at the airfield were war-weary P-39 Airacobras. The squadron, under the command of Robert Tresville, flew its first missions in the P-39 that day. Meanwhile, the 301st (led by Charles DeBow) and the 302nd (with Edward Gleed in command) flew their first missions from Montecorvino two days later.

Flying coastal patrol sorties in second-hand P-39s was not what the group had expected. This assignment required pilots to monitor an area from Cape Palermo and the Gulf of Policastro to the Ponziane Islands. Davis referred to this tasking as 'a slap in the face', and flying over the ocean in worn-out fighters was dangerous even when there was no sign of the enemy.

'We went over there and we were really excited', said Samuel Curtis. 'We were going into battle and we were going to really show them. Then we had our first casualty'. After suffering an engine failure, Clemenceau Givings of the 100th FS bailed out of his P-39 but drowned in Naples Harbour after becoming entangled in his parachute. 'I'll never forget the fellow, because he was the life of the squadron', Curtis recalled. 'He was a lively kind of guy, and he was the first one lost. One day we came back and they said "Clem got killed", and it came as a real shock. It was then we realised we were really in a war zone'.

Lt Samuel Curtis was a graduate of TAAF Class 43-G, and as such, he was amongst the first pilots to join the 332nd FG. Having survived the P-39 and P-47, he went on to fly many escort missions in the P-51B/C (*Jon Lake Collection*)

Ed Gleed began the war as CO of the 302nd FS, but he was relieved by Lt Col Benjamin O Davis after an ill-conceived strafing mission that led to the loss of a P-39 and injuries to its pilot. Gleed later redeemed himself with a two-kill haul on 27 July 1944, and ended the war as group operations officer – he is seen here in the latter capacity briefing an up-and-coming escort mission for the 332nd FG (*National Museum of the USAF*)

On 15 February, the group discovered how unsuited its Airacobras were for combat. Roy Spencer and William Melton of the 302nd FS spotted a Ju 88 flying a reconnaissance mission near Ponsa Point, at the mouth of Naples Harbour. Both men succeeding in damaging the German aircraft, yet the Ju 88 was still able to both climb and accelerate away from its frustrated pursuers.

Six days later, the 100th FS moved to Capodichino airfield, from which the 99th FS was still operating as part of the 79th FG. While the latter unit was engaged in Operation *Strangle*, the 332nd was still assigned to the lowly task of harbour patrol. Bored of these missions, and without Davis' permission, Tresville and Gleed worked out a patrol route that would take them near to the Anzio beachhead, where they hoped to find German fighters.

Davis was furious when he found out and gave Tresville a dressing down, but Gleed, ever the aggressive go-getter, scheduled another identical mission – 16 fighters took off and headed north toward the beachhead, then turned inland. Gleed had to turn back because of engine trouble with his P-39, but Wendell Pruitt, who was operations officer for the 302nd FS, continued on towards Rome, where fuel started to run low.

The P-39s' straight-line course back to Capodichino took them through the flak corridor between Rome and the beachhead, and Walter Westmoreland's P-39L (42-4478) was shot out from under him. Westmoreland bailed out but broke his leg in the process. As a result of this unapproved mission, an angry Davis relieved Gleed of command of the 302nd and sent him to the 301st. Melvin 'Red' Jackson assumed command of the 302nd.

VOLCANIC ERUPTION

On 15 March Mt Vesuvius' eruption layered Capodichino in fine ash, bringing a pause to the aerial action from the base. The lasting effect of this natural disaster was the presence of smoke and ash in the air for several weeks that, according to Walter Palmer of the 100th FS, forced patrols to fly north of the main volcanic plume beyond the harbour, before turning back towards the Anzio beachhead.

These conditions also posed safety hazards in unexpected ways, as 2Lt Virgil Richardson discovered when he landed following a patrol and only then spotted a flock of ash-covered sheep wandering across the runway. Richardson's P-39 hit the animals, causing the nose gear strut to snap. 'Then, the gas tank, located directly under my seat, caught fire', Richardson told historian Ben Vinson III. 'Let me tell you that there is nothing that can make you move faster than having a live fire under your ass!'

Richardson pulled the handle on the door, which fell off. As he stepped onto the wing of the skidding aeroplane, it veered to the right, throwing him to the ground. Luckily, he landed on his dinghy, which broke his fall. Even so, Richardson's injuries kept him flat on his back for three weeks, followed by a lengthy recuperation at the rest camp in Naples.

Two days after the eruption, the harbour patrols were up and running again. Laurence Wilkins and Weldon K Groves spotted another Ju 88 making the daily reconnaissance run over the Naples area and, despite holing the aircraft's wing, Wilkins and Groves could only watch as the Junkers used superior speed to escape once again.

By 15 April, the headquarters unit of the 332nd FG and the 301st and 302nd FSs had departed Montecorvino and joined the 100th FS at Capodichino. The latter base was far more comfortable, with an electrical generator chief among its amenities. Unfortunately, the airfield was also a magnet for Luftwaffe bombers, which staged a nuisance raid on 19 April that did no harm. Sadly, the same could not be said of the P-39s, for 2Lt Beryl Wyatt of the 100th FS

A 332nd FG P-39 with some interesting door art serves as a backdrop for a war bond poster published in the summer of 1944. Although the mainstream US press was not eager to cover black fighter units, the government had few qualms about using the image of black pilots to lure money from their fellow black Americans at home (*Lt Col Harold C Hayes Collection*)

died a few hours later when his misfiring fighter crashed whilst on a patrol. The following day, group public relations officer Lt Ray Ware informed the pilots that they would soon be converting to the P-47D, much to the glee of the men.

The Luftwaffe returned to Capodichino on the morning of 21 April on yet another nuisance raid. Just as the group was learning to ignore these nocturnal visitations, the base was bombed again on the 24th by 30-40 Ju 88s. The 30-minute attack caused more damage than previous raids, and inspired new enthusiasm for the once-onerous task of foxhole-digging. Later that same day, the group launched a strafing mission, but on take-off the P-39 of 2Lt Edgar Jones of the 100th FS went out of control and the pilot was killed in the ensuing crash. The P-47s could not arrive soon enough.

On 25 April the first six Thunderbolts flew in to Capodichino, these aircraft being hand-me-downs from the 325th FG. The Thunderbolts were distributed evenly between all three squadrons, and their yellow-and-black checkered tails repainted all red – the new group colour.

Harbour patrol missions continued to dominate the group's activities, with occasional strafing sorties thrown in. Strafing in the P-39 could be a hazardous undertaking, as the fighter's liquid-cooled Allison engine was vulnerable to even the smallest shell fragment (one hit and the powerplant would lose its vital coolant and seize up in just a matter of minutes), and

the Anzio area was teeming with German flak. And just to prove how deadly the guns were, on 5 May 1Lt James R Polkinghorne of the 301st was shot down and killed in his P-39 during a strafing mission.

Capodichino remained a temptation for German raiders into the spring of 1944, and from 14 May onwards, the Luftwaffe regularly appeared in the night sky between 0300 and 0400 hrs, causing little damage but disturbing the group's sleep.

Five days later, the group received an additional ten P-47s and started transition training in earnest. Even these sorties could be hazardous, however, and on 22 May 2Lt Henry Pollard (who, in civilian life, had been a well-known saxophone player with the Jimmy Lunceford Orchestra) was killed when his P-47D (42-75826) crashed near Casalnuovo during transition training. Pollard, who had been with the group just three weeks, became the first 302nd FS pilot lost in Italy.

Meanwhile, the Airacobras also continued to exact a toll. On 24 May the 301st lost 1Lt John Henry Prowell Jnr when his P-39L (42-4537) crashed during a convoy protection mission, and nine days later Elmer 'Chubby' Taylor's Airacobra caught fire over the harbour. He bailed out, but his parachute failed to open and Taylor plunged to his death.

On 26 May Lt Woodrow Morgan was shot down and captured during a strafing mission in P-47D 42-75830. An even more ignominious fate befell 2Lt Lloyd S Hathcock of the 301st, who became disoriented during a flight three days later in P-47D 42-75971. Landing at Rome-Littorio airfield, which was still occupied by the Germans, Hathcock was quickly captured and his Thunderbolt, after having its wingtips and cowling painted yellow (Luftwaffe theatre colours), was despatched north to the Rechlin Test Centre for evaluation.

Groundcrews of the 332nd FG are instructed on the identifying features of the RAF's Short Stirling bomber with the aid of models built by schoolchildren in the USA. For most of the enlisted men, visual identification was a moot point, for the Luftwaffe typically paid its visits in the dead on night (*Western Aerospace Museum*)

Ex-301st FS P-47D-16 42-75971 is seen abandoned at Göttingen, in Germany, soon after VE-Day. This aircraft was landed in error at Rome-Littorio airfield by Lt Lloyd S Hathcock on 29 May 1944 after the pilot became disoriented during a ferry mission from Foggia Main to Ramitelli airfields. The P-47 was duly sent to Germany and maintained in an airworthy condition until the final weeks of the conflict in Europe (*Eddie Creek Collection*)

In October 1944 the Thunderbolt was transferred to the famous *Zirkus Rosarius*, whose job it was to familiarise Luftwaffe units with the strengths and weaknesses of enemy fighter types through mock combat with captured aircraft. Hatchcock's P-47D was the first of its type to fall into enemy hands with fully functioning water injection, and the aircraft was kept airworthy well into 1945. It was eventually found abandoned, minus its propeller and sitting on its tail, at Göttingen airfield when the base was captured by US troops in the final weeks of the war in Europe.

According to Lt Alexander Jefferson, who met Lloyd Hathcock in a PoW camp after his own P-51 had been shot down by flak in August 1944, 'He will never live down the fact that he landed at a German air base due to a navigational error. Their base was 35 miles in one direction and ours 35 miles in the opposite direction. Was he surprised when his groundcrew spoke German and had white faces!'

These events soured the ending of the 332nd's initial period of operations. On 27 May, an advance echelon of the 332nd headquarters group moved to Ramitelli. Four days later, the group was detached from the Twelfth Air Force and attached to the Fifteenth Air Force, freeing it from harbour patrols and placing it immediately in the thick of the strategic bombing campaign, which was being waged deep inside German-held territory.

TO WAR IN THE THUNDERBOLT

Col Benjamin Davis wasted little time in getting his newly-equipped squadrons into the air. On 7 June, 32 P-47s conducted a fighter sweep of the Ferrara-Bologna area, finding little activity other than sporadic flak. During the flight to the target area, 2Lt Carroll N Langston Jnr's instruments indicated that he was losing oil pressure and he bailed out. A search was launched, but Langston was never recovered. Other pilots reported their oil pressure gauges also mistakenly indicated low pressure, and groundcrews made a concerted effort to repair the gauges, thus solving an innocuous problem that had cost a pilot his life.

The next day, the 332nd launched a 32-aeroplane escort for 5th Bomb Wing (BW) B-17s that were sent to attack targets in the Italian city of Pola (now Pula, in Croatia) – the group's first strategic bomber mission escort.

Col Davis had vehemently stressed to his pilots at the briefing that the group had to protect the bombers at all costs. He scorned other fighter groups' tactics, stating that 'as soon as the bombers reached the target area, they'd peel off and go looking for targets of opportunity. We didn't do that. We went through the target area, and if there were any cripples coming off the target we would assign an element – two fighters – to escort that cripple to a base where he could land safely'. The group flew close escort, Davis said, with 12- or 16-aeroplane squadron formations flying slow turns over the bombers.

While the Pola escort proved uneventful, the mission flown 48 hours later was anything but. At 0700 hrs, 39 P-47s of the 301st and 302nd FSs departed Ramitelli (with three aborts) and rendezvoused with the 5th, 49th, 55th, 57th and 304th BWs, which were headed for targets in the Munich area.

As the formation neared Udine, four Bf 109s made a diving attack on a group of Liberators, triggering a swirling dogfight. After the Bf 109s made their firing pass, they turned to the left and Lt Wendell Pruitt latched onto one of them. 'As the Jerries passed under me, I rolled over, shoved everything forward, dove and closed on one (a Bf 109G) at 475 mph', he reported. 'I gave him a short burst of machine gun fire, and discovering that I was giving him too much lead, I waited as he shallowed out of a turn. Then I gave two long two-second bursts. His left wing erupted in flames'. Pruitt's wingman saw the German pilot bail out and the Bf 109 explode when it slammed into the ground.

At about the same time, 'Red' Jackson spotted five or six Bf 109s at '11 o'clock high' and closed with them. He fired on one fighter, which started to descend in a spin. Jackson, having lost his flight in his pursuit of the spinning Bf 109, then had another Messerschmitt make a head-on pass at him. He pulled up and the P-47 stalled, allowing the Bf 109 to get on his tail. Meanwhile, Lt Charles Bussey's formation of eight P-47s latched onto the tail of the four remaining Bf 109s, including the one chasing Jackson.

Lt William Green fired on Jackson's pursuer, then Bussey opened up on the same Bf 109, blowing the tail off the German fighter. Bussey's wingman saw the pilot bail out and the aeroplane explode in mid-air. Bussey and Green were each given a share in the kill.

Jackson, unaware of the action behind him, used his P-47's injected water boost to scoot into some low clouds in an effort to evade his now-despatched pursuer. As he emerged from the clouds, Jackson saw another Bf 109 at '11 o'clock' and turned into it, eventually getting into a firing position and putting a burst into the fighter's belly. 'Metal flew off his left side', Jackson later recalled. 'The Nazi pilot bailed out over a German airfield. I hit the deck and came home'.

Frederick Funderberg, meanwhile, spotted two Bf 109s 500 ft below him at his 'nine o'clock'. He and his wingman peeled off to engage them and Funderberg fired a quick burst, causing pieces to come off of one of the Bf 109s. As his flight passed below the two German fighters and started to pull up for another pass, they came face-to-face with a second

During the 332nd's five-kill day on 9 June 1944, which provided the group with its only aerial victories with the P-47, Frederick Funderberg scored two of them. Funderberg served with the 301st FS until 29 December 1944, when he and Andrew Marshall disappeared over Passau. They had fallen victim either to flak or a mid-air collision (*Lt Col Harold C Hayes Collection*)

Floyd Rayford, John W Rogers and Spann Watson pose next to the runway at Ramitelli. Rayford was wounded by flak during the 9 June 1944 mission, but recovered and eventually took command of the 301st FS (*National Air and Space Museum*)

pair of Messerschmitts. Funderberg fired off a quick burst and the P-47's eight machine guns tore one of the German fighters apart. Other pilots in Funderberg's flight saw two aircraft splash into the Adriatic, as well as a single parachute, far below them.

Elsewhere, Lt Robert Wiggins spied yet another Bf 109 to his left at about his altitude, so he turned into him and attacked. A full-deflection shot caused pieces of the fighter to fly off, but its pilot put the smoking aeroplane into a shallow dive to gain speed and climbed away.

The day's five kills were not without loss, however, as Cornelius Rogers, flying P-47D 42-75800, was killed, and the aircraft of Capt Floyd Rayford and Lt William Hunter received flak damage, with Rayford picking up a superficial wound in the process.

Back at Ramitelli, representatives from Republic and senior officers from Fifteenth Air Force HQ were lecturing the pilots not assigned to fly that day about the peculiarities of the P-47. A major stood on a truck telling the assembled pilots, whom he referred to as 'boys', that the Thunderbolt should never be slow-rolled below 1000 ft because of its excessive weight.

As if on cue, Lts Wendell Pruitt and Lee Archer, known by the squadron as 'the Gruesome Twosome', came screaming across the field on the deck, wingtip-to-wingtip, at the end of the escort mission. They pulled up and threw their P-47s into slow victory rolls. Aghast, the indignant major screamed at the two Thunderbolts 'You can't do that!'

MORE MISSIONS

After a two-day break, the 301st and 302nd FSs put up 30 P-47s to cover the 5th and 55th BWs' raid on Smedervo, in Yugoslavia, on 11 June, followed on the 13th by a 32-aeroplane mission by the same two squadrons escorting the 5th and 49th BWs to the Munich area. On the latter mission, the Luftwaffe once again put in an appearance near Udine, but of the 11 fighters seen, only four pressed home their attacks. One P-47 was damaged, but the bombers were protected.

The Luftwaffe's response was even less enthusiastic during the 14 June mission to Budapest, in Hungary. The 301st and 302nd sent up 29 P-47s to escort the 5th, 49th, 55th and 304th BWs, and although 15 Bf 109s and

Capt Robert Tresville left West Point a year early to go to flight school and take command of the 100th FS. A combination of a long low-level flight and strange weather conditions contributed to his death on 27 June 1944, when his P-47 was one of four to crash into the Tyrrhenian Sea (*Lt Col Harold C Hayes Collection*)

Lt Willard Woods also came close to crashing during the ill-fated 27 June 1944 low-level mission over the Tyrrhenian Sea. He later went on to complete his tour in this P-51C, marked up with an Ace of Clubs motif beneath the cockpit. Note the ring and bead gunsight affixed to the windscreen framing directly in the pilot's eyeline (*Jon Lake Collection*)

seven twin-engined fighters were spotted, they made no effort to attack the bombers, or their P-47 escorts.

The long-range missions continued on the 16th, when the 100th, 301st and 302nd FSs covered a maximum-effort bombing raid against targets in the Bratislava area – 40 P-47s escorted the bombers from Banja Luka, in Yugoslavia, to the target. Six days later, the same three squadrons provided escort for another maximum-strength raid to Bucharest-Giurgiu, in Rumania. Both missions passed without incident.

The uneventful trips north came to an end on 23 June, much to the group's sorrow. The day's orders called for Capt Robert Tresville to lead 41 P-47s from the 100th, 301st and 302nd FSs on a low-level strafing attack of the strategically placed Airasca-Pinerolo landing ground, which was little more than a mile west of Airasca in the Piedmont region of northwestern Italy.

From the start, the mission was beset by problems. Gwynne Peirson's P-47D 42-75772 crashed on take-off, but the pilot survived. Four other P-47s were forced to abort, leaving 36 Thunderbolts in formation to cross the Tyrrhenian Sea at less than 100 ft in order to take the airfield, and its occupants, by surprise.

The weather was described as hazy over the water, with a very bright glare from the sun and a cloud base of just 1000 ft. Near Cape Corse, with the pilots finding it very difficult to discern the horizon, 2Lt Sam Jefferson's aeroplane dropped too low, touched the water and exploded on impact. At almost the same time Earl Sherrard's P-47 pancaked into the water – he scrambled out of his fighter and was later rescued. 2Lt Charles B Johnson, who was circling Sherrard's machine in order to check that the pilot was still alive, also flew into the water. He was unable to escape from his cockpit before the P-47 sank, however.

A few minutes later, the lead element experienced the effects of the strange weather. Tresville, flying with Dempsey Morgan and Spurgeon Ellington as the second section in his flight, frantically gestured at wingman Willard L Woods to pull up – the latter was so close to the water that his wing tanks were starting to kick up rooster-tails.

Just after they sighted the coast, according to Woods, Tresville's own P-47 struck the water, which stripped off the drop tanks, ripped off the ailerons and bent the propeller back over the cowling. The Thunderbolt bounced back into the air momentarily, but then slammed back into the water, leaving only its tail visible. Woods later reported that Tresville was looking at a map when he crashed.

The group never found the target – radio silence prevented the deputy formation leader from learning of Tresville's crash, and kept him from assuming navigational responsibilities for the attack.

The loss of Tresville, who, like Col Davis, was another rare black West Pointer, was keenly felt by the group. 'Tresville was a fantastic guy', said Samuel Curtis. 'He was smart, he was bright, he was strong, he was well-coordinated. He would have gone far'. Andrew 'Jug' Turner assumed command of the 100th FS upon Tresville's death

On 23 June the group escorted a mission to Sofia, in Bulgaria, and saw no opposition, but two days later it would accomplish one of its more unique feats. The 100th, 301st and 302nd FSs were despatched to attack troops in Yugoslavia, sending 20 P-47s out in five flights. One four-ship flight became a two-ship flight when Freddie Hutchins' left drop tank refused to come off, forcing he and wingman Larry Wilkins to return early to Ramitelli. The other two pilots in the flight, Wendell Pruitt and Gwynne Peirson, continued on, but strong winds forced the fighters off course and they missed the reported location of the troop concentration.

Dejectedly, Pruitt and Peirson set a course for home that carried them over the Italian port city of Trieste. There before them in the harbour,

Col Benjamin O Davis was leading the group on the day (9 June 1944) it scored its Thunderbolt kills. While Davis despatched two flights to deal with the enemy fighters, he kept the rest of his aeroplanes with the bombers – a tactic that would earn the group the admiration of many bomber crews (*National Museum of the USAF*)

steaming towards the open sea, was what they identified as a German destroyer – a black cross was clearly visible on its funnel. Pruitt and Peirson, flying side by side, opened fire. Pruitt's rounds struck the ship, which in actuality was the German-operated ex-Italian torpedo boat TA-27 (now used as a mine-layer). The vessel soon began to burn, and the smoke attracted the attention of Joseph Elsberry, Joseph Lewis and Charles Dunne, who joined Pruitt and Peirson in their strafing attacks.

On Peirson's second pass, his rounds apparently struck one of the vessel's mines, for it was engulfed by a massive explosion. When the debris cleared, the pilots were rewarded with the sight of the ship rolling over and sinking near Pirano. The group also strafed radar/radio stations around the harbour, shot up trucks and the wharf at Muggio, and sank a sailing boat that fired on them off Isola. Peirson landed with several jagged holes in the undersides of his wings, which he suspected were caused by debris thrown into the air by the ship's explosion. He and Pruitt were awarded DFCs for the action.

The 99th FS never flew the P-47 in combat, but pilots will be pilots! Proving the point, the 99th's Capt Ed Toppins smiles from the cockpit of a war-weary Thunderbolt at Ramitelli. Having completed his combat tour in the MTO, Toppins was later killed in an aircraft accident at Tuskegee Army Air Field on 17 March 1945 (*Herman Lawson via the National Museum of the USAF*)

The day after the group's destroyer-busting mission, 36 Thunderbolts escorted a maximum effort to the Lake Balaton area of Hungary. Two of the flight leaders were forced to abandon their fighters due to mechanical problems with their combat-weary P-47Ds. Lt Andrew Maples bailed out near Termoli, on the outbound leg, and was rescued, but Lt Maurice V Esters, who took to his parachute near Vetacandrija, was never seen again.

On 27 June, a 37-aeroplane force escorted the 5th and 47th BWs to Budapest, and while there were no combat losses, the Thunderbolts of Larry Wilkins and Washington Ross were damaged in a collision soon after landing. The next day saw an identical number of aircraft escort the 304th BW to the Ferdinand area of northern Italy. On take-off, Lt Edward Laird was killed when his P-47 left the runway and crashed, and Lt Mac Ross survived an emergency landing at Lecce airfield. Lt Alfonso Davis' P-47 had suffered a blown tyre on take-off, and on the way back from the mission, he made a successful forced landing in a field near Otranto. Finally, Lt Floyd Thompson was forced to take to his parachute near Forli, and he was immediately taken prisoner by the Germans.

The last day of June saw the 100th, 301st and 302nd FSs mount an escort mission for five bomb wings sent to attack targets in the Vienna area. Forty-five P-47s took off, and there were just two aborts – a vast improvement from the mechanical woes of the 27th. The mission proceeded without any hitches.

Although the group had by now started to receive unpainted 'bubbletop' P-47D-30s to complement its older 'razorbacks', the 30 June mission would prove to be its final one in the Thunderbolt – the 332nd had begun to receive P-51B/Cs in late June. And like the Thunderbolts before them, these aircraft were also 'hand-me-downs' from the 31st and 325th FGs.

In just 30 days of P-47 action, the group had destroyed five aeroplanes and an enemy vessel. More significantly, its pilots had learned the intricacies of conducting effective close bomber escort missions. The experience would pay dividends, both for the 332nd FG and the bomber crews that it would escort over coming months.

ENTER THE MUSTANG

While the 332nd FG was flying its final missions in the P-39 and mastering the P-47, the 99th FS and its war-weary P-40Ls had moved to a new base at Pignataro on 10 May, then transferred across to Ciampo Field and Orbetelo for brief stays. On 3 July, the squadron finally moved to Ramitelli and officially joined the 332nd FG – a move seen by some in the 99th as a less than positive one.

Many pilots in the unit saw the new group as being green and inexperienced, and resented being forced to fly with it. Others viewed it as a step back toward segregation, for instead of flying as a component within a white group, they had again been lumped together in an all-black unit.

Conversely, the men of the 332nd FG feared that the group's leadership roles would be handed over to more experienced pilots from the 99th FS, but this did not come to pass. From an administrative standpoint, this merger created a four-squadron group – a rarity in the USAAF that placed additional pressure on the group commander. To make matters worse, Tuskegee Army Air Field was unable to produce enough pilots for all four squadrons and the then-forming 477th Medium Bombardment Group, meaning that combat tours were far longer than in other groups.

Things were not all bad, however. By July 1944, the 332nd had replaced all of its Thunderbolts with P-51B/C Mustangs, and these aircraft were far better suited to the long-range escort missions that the group was being assigned by the Fifteenth Air Force. The fighter's added range and speed were welcome advantages.

Still, the transition from one aircraft to another was not without peril, and Othell Dickson, a stand-out in training, was killed while performing aerobatics over Ramitelli when his Mustang plunged to earth during an inverted manoeuvre. Speculation centred on the fuselage fuel tank – when full, it could adversely affect the centre of gravity and make recovery from manoeuvres like Dickson's impossible.

The arrival of the Mustang coincided with Col Benjamin Davis' difficult decision to relieve Charles DeBow as commander of the 301st and replace him with Lee Rayford,

Mac Ross was a member of Tuskegee's first class, but sentimentality did not prevent classmate Benjamin O Davis from relieving him as the 301st FS's operations officer. On 10 July 1944, Ross' Mustang entered a shallow dive and slammed into a hill, killing him. Rumours that the crash was a suicide persist, although the nature of the accident suggests that an oxygen system failure may have claimed his life (*Lt Col Harold C Hayes Collection*)

who was a combat veteran from the 99th who had just returned for a second tour. DeBow had failed to meet Davis' expectations for 'leadership in the air', the commanding officer stated. Davis also relieved fellow Tuskegee classmate Mac Ross as the squadron's operations officer.

Still, the Mustangs lifted the group's morale, and as a visible sign of confidence, groundcrews applied the group marking of a solid red tail to all of their fighters. 'We wanted the American bombers to know we were escorting them', said Herbert Carter. 'The red tails would also let the German interceptors know who was escorting the bombers'.

On 4 July 1944, the 332nd flew its first mission with the Mustang – a 40-aeroplane escort of the 5th and 47th BWs. Col Davis led the flight, but turned over command to Lt Claude Govan when his radios malfunctioned. 5 July saw the 100th, 301st and 302nd provide 52 P-51s for an escort mission. All aircraft returned safely, although fuel forced four to land on Corsica. The group sighted two Bf 109s, but the Germans made no attempt to attack the bombers, and they failed to lure the escorting Mustangs away from their charges. On 6 July, 37 P-51s escorted the 47th BW to Latisana and Tagliamento/Casarsa, and the very next day 47 Mustangs covered a raid on Vienna. All returned safely.

While the junior squadrons of the group were flying missions, the 99th FS received its first P-51B/Cs. On 8 July the old hands worked to master the fighter's intricacies.

The rest of the group, meanwhile, was itching to tangle with the Luftwaffe, and on the 8th one of them would. The 100th, 301st and 302nd had sent 46 Mustangs to escort the 304th BW to Munchendorf airfield, and the attack drew 15 to 20 German fighters into the air. Before they could be engaged by the 332nd, however, they were intercepted by a group of P-38s. One Bf 109 made it through the Lightnings and attacked Lt Earl S Sherrard over the target. Sherrard wrung out his P-51 in an effort to elude the Bf 109, finally shaking him after a long-running encounter.

Clarence Dart, Elwood T Driver, Heber Houston and Alva Temple of the 99th re-live the day's combat in this staged photo from the summer of 1944. Temple and Driver served two tours with the 99th FS

Joseph Elsberry poses with his P-51C *Joedebelle* after his three-kill mission on 12 July 1944. Elsberry scored three and a probable that day (all officially unconfirmed), and later tallied another kill, putting him tantalisingly close to ace status. Note the taped-over ammunition tray edges on the wing (lower left)

Unfortunately, just as the Bf 109 disappeared from sight Sherrard was attacked by the P-38s, and he was forced to repeat his evasive manoeuvres. After eluding the Lightnings, Sherrard landed his Mustang at a forward field, pilot and fuel both exhausted.

On 9 July, 32 P-51s from the 100th, 301st and 302nd FSs escorted the 47th BW to the Concordia Vega Oil Refineries at Ploesti, in Rumania – it would become a frequent destination for the group. Two Bf 109s and two Fw 190s were spotted, but again they were intercepted by P-51s from another fighter group.

Meanwhile, the 99th FS was struggling to master the Mustang. On 10 July, Mac Ross, who had been relieved as group operations officer just a few days earlier, died when the P-51B (42-106552) he was checking out entered a slow, shallow descent and eventually hit the side of a hill. There was little physical evidence to explain the accident – an oxygen system failure seemed to be the likely cause. The next day, during a transition flight in P-51C 42-103913, Capt Leon Roberts (the last member of the original 99th FS still with the unit) plunged into the ocean from high altitude. Again, speculation centred on a possible case of hypoxia. At the time of his death, Roberts had flown no fewer than 116 combat sorties.

That same day, the group began a series of missions to soften up southern France. The 100th, 301st and 302nd sent 33 P-51s on an uneventful mission to escort 47th BW 'heavies' attacking the submarine pens at Toulon. On 12 July, while escorting B-24s of the 49th BW on a mission to destroy railway marshalling yards in southern France, some 25 German fighters jumped the 332nd over the French coast. After the fray, flight leader Joseph Elsberry claimed three kills and a probable, although for some reason his victories went unconfirmed.

Elsberry's first victim made a pass on the bombers and was turning away when he hit him with a 30-degree deflection shot, resulting in the Fw 190 streaming heavy black smoke and falling off to the left. Next, Elsberry spotted a second Focke-Wulf that turned in front and below him, and he put his Mustang into a 30-degree dive, quickly closing on the hapless fighter. Elsberry started firing and hit the Fw 190's left wing, causing the German fighter to commence to slow roll. He continued to fire short bursts at his quarry until it slammed into the ground during a 'split-S' manoeuvre.

The victorious pilot climbed to re-enter the fight, and was rewarded by the sight of a third Fw 190 turning away from him as if to make its escape. Elsberry drew a lead on the German fighter and fired a two-second burst that arced into his target, sending it crashing into the ground, as witnessed by Lts Dunne and Friend.

As Elsberry pulled off this target, another Fw 190 shot by in a 45-degree dive, so he flung the Mustang to the right and followed the aeroplane down. With only his left wing guns firing, Elsberry gave his Mustang *Joedebelle* a boot-full of right rudder so as to keep his sights on the fleeing Fw 190 and opened fire, scoring hits across the enemy aeroplane's left wing root. The Fw 190 started spiralling down, and soon straightened into a dive, but its pilot never recovered and the Focke-Wulf crashed on French soil.

Meanwhile, Harold Sawyer scored a confirmed kill over Nimes by destroying an Fw 190 after it made an attack on the bomber stream. Six German fighters had dived through the Liberators, then 'split-S'ed' away, turned left, then 'split-S'ed' again. Sawyer fired a burst at the trailing aircraft, which never pulled out of its second 'split-S' and slammed into the ground. Sawyer immediately spotted a second Fw 190 lining up to attack the bombers from about 'ten o'clock', and he gunned down this fighter as well, although the latter kill was not confirmed. Lt George Rhodes was shot down during the battle, bailing out near Viterbo, but he was rescued and returned to the squadron.

Charley Haynes, James Sheppard and Frank Bradley prepare to secure an empty 75-gallon tank to the right wing pylon of a P-51B. External tanks were a must, because many missions required the Mustangs to cross the Italian Alps (*National Museum of the USAF*)

13 July brought a return to Italian targets, with the 100th, 301st and 302nd sending 37 P-51s to escort two groups from the 5th BW sent to attack the Pinzano railway bridge and the Vinzone viaduct. Two days later, the 99th flew with the group's three other squadrons for the first time during a raid on the refineries at Ploesti. The 55th BW had an escort of 61 P-51s, which earned kudos from the bomber crews by chasing off eight Bf 109s that were harassing three straggling 'heavies' near Krusevac.

Col Davis continued to drill home the message that the group's primary mission was to stay with the bombers, even if it meant 'protecting them with your life'. While this grated with some of the fighter pilots, none dared disobey the colonel.

MACCHI MENACE

16 July found 45 Mustangs from the 100th, 301st and 302nd getting a chance to range free on a fighter sweep over Vienna. The group chanced upon a single Macchi C.205 fighter creeping up on a straggling B-24 from the bomber's 'five o'clock low' position in a gradual climbing turn.

Although Italy had switched sides in 1943, there were still fascist Italians flying for the *Aviazone Nationale Republicana* (ANR) of Mussolini's rump state, the Italian Socialist Republic. Formation leader Lt Alfonso Davis of the 302nd FS ordered his flight of four Mustangs to intercept the Macchi. As they dived on the fighter, Lt Davis overshot, but his wingman, Lt William 'Chubby' Green, turned inside the C.205 and fired a series of bursts that caused the Italian fighter to stream black smoke.

Green followed his foe almost to the deck before the Macchi pilot tried to make a low-altitude turn around a mountain – the disabled fighter caught a wingtip on the mountainside and cartwheeled into a fireball. Meanwhile, Davis had climbed to cover Green, and he spotted a second Macchi about 5000 ft below him. Davis dived on the fighter, catching it in a left turn. A 60-degree deflection shot caused chunks of the fuselage to fly off, before the Macchi fell into a spin to the left and crashed.

The next day, the group returned to southern France, escorting the 306th BW on a bombing mission to the Avignon railway marshalling yard and railway bridge in southern France. Again, the Mustang pilots found the hunting good, with 19 Bf 109s rising to challenge the formation. Only three chose to attack the bombers, however, running in at the B-24s in a line-astern formation from their 'eight o'clock' position. They 'split-S'ed' away at the sight of the P-51s descending on them, and then made a series of evasive left turns. Three pilots – Luther 'Quibbling' Smith, Robert 'Dissipatin'' Smith and Larry Wilkins – closed in and methodically despatched their victims, following them all the way down to their final impacts with the ground.

2Lt Maceo Harris was also in the thick of things. 'My flight leader and I went down on two bogies, and after they "split-S'ed" from me at about 18,000 ft, I pulled up all alone in a tight chandelle to the left', he reported. 'I tried to join another ship, but lost him when I peeled off on two more bogies that were after some bombers. The bogies turned steeply to the left, and P-51s were in the vicinity, so I kept on with the bombers because they were hitting the target. Flak was intense over the target, and I kept an eye on the B-24s for enemy fighters that might come in when the bombers left the area.

Clarence 'Lucky' Lester's three kills on 18 July 1944 came after his flight leader spotted Bf 109s above their formation. After punching off his tanks, 'I closed to about 200 ft and started to fire', he subsequently wrote. 'Smoke began to pour out of the Me 109 and the aircraft exploded. I was going so fast I was sure that I would hit some of the debris, but luckily I didn't'. Almost immediately, Lester saw another Bf 109 to his right. He latched onto the fighter's tail and opened fire. 'His aircraft started to smoke', said Lester. 'I looked down to see the enemy pilot emerge from his burning aircraft. I remember seeing his blond hair as he bailed out'. By now alone, Lester spotted a Bf 109 at 1000 ft. He dived on it and opened fire – as his rounds struck, the Bf 109 pilot panicked and 'split-S'ed' into the ground (*National Museum of the USAF*)

'Upon leaving the target, I joined another P-51 and tried to contact him by radio', Harris continued. 'My attempt was unsuccessful, so I peeled off alone on three bogies who were approaching a straggling bomber from the rear. They looked like P-51s, and I rocked my wings coming in, but they swung left over France away from the bomber.

'I widely circled the B-24 because the top turret gunner was firing at me, but when he stopped firing I came in very close to survey the flak damage. The number two engine was feathered and the number one was smoking moderately.'

The B-24's compass was shot out, and while Harris could receive the bomber on radio, it could not receive him. He used hand signals to

The crew of 'Lucky' Lester's Mustang finds some shelter from the Italian sun in the shadow of the aeroplane's wing. Lester's three-kill day on 18 July over Udine represented his only aerial victories (*Frank Ambrose*)

'Lucky' Lester and his crew chief admire the freshly-applied victory symbols beneath the cockpit of *Miss-Pelt*. This particular Mustang was purchased in part through $75,000 in donations from the students and teachers of the Sisters of Notre Dame's Alphonsius School in Chicago, which was Lester's home town (*National Museum of the USAF*)

indicate that the two aeroplanes would be over Corsica in 40 minutes, and put the B-24 on course. When Harris could not raise 'Blacktop' (the control tower on Corsica), he buzzed the airstrip several times to clear the runway. The B-24 made a two-wheel recovery, and Harris landed as well. 'The B-24 pilot was Lt Loerb from San Francisco', said Harris. 'He is in the 459th BG and his ship is No 129585. He and the co-pilot appreciated my friendly aid, and kissed me after the manner of the French'.

1Lt Walter Palmer's day was equally eventful. Taking off through cloud cover, he circled over Ramitelli but failed to spot the rest of his flight, so he decided to catch up with them on his own.

Once over southern France, Palmer spotted an aeroplane heading in the opposite direction, rocking its wings. He rocked his wings in return, but instead of joining up from the side, the aircraft tried to 'join up' from behind. Palmer kept his eyes on his new 'wingman' and was not entirely surprised when he saw flashes from its guns. He threw his Mustang into a turn and identified the other aeroplane as a Bf 109. After a series of turns, the German flyer realised that Palmer was getting close to a firing position, so he 'split-S'ed' for the deck. Palmer wisely set course for home, with a stop in Corsica for fuel.

On 18 July, Lee Rayford led 66 Mustangs from all four squadrons to the briefed rendezvous point over southern Germany, but the bombers of the 5th BW, scheduled to strike the Luftwaffe base at Memmingen, in Austria, were nowhere to be found. Rayford decided to orbit in the Udine-Treviso area, which was already known to be a hotbed of Luftwaffe activity, and as the bombers approached, the Mustang pilots spotted a swarm of 30 to 35 Bf 109s to the right of the formation. The fighters attacked in groups from 'three o'clock high' and 'five o'clock low', then 'split-S'ed' away. Twenty-one of the Mustangs rushed to break up the attack, destroying 11 of the German fighters.

Once this threat had been dealt with, the formation continued to Austria, but over the target, 30 to 40 enemy aeroplanes – mainly Bf 109s, Fw 190s and Me 410s – were sighted. Eventually, four Fw 190s swooped in to attack and two were shot down.

The tally for the day was impressive, with Clarence 'Lucky' Lester bagging three, Jack Holsclaw two and Lee Archer, Charles Bailey, Walter

302nd FS pilot, and future ace, Lt Lee 'Buddy' Archer claimed a solitary kill on 18 July 1944 (*Lt Col Lee Archer Collection*)

Palmer, Roger Romine, Edward Toppins and Hugh Warner one apiece. Palmer's victim was a Bf 109, which he hit with several short bursts after it had made a pass at the bombers. 'On the second or third burst I noticed his engine smoking heavily, so I broke it off because there were others to shoot down', he later wrote. Palmer closed in on a second Bf 109, but his guns jammed. He considered chopping off the enemy fighter's tail with his propeller, but the Bf 109 headed into a cloud bank shrouding the tops of the Alps, convincing Palmer to break off the pursuit.

Toppins destroyed his opponent by diving at him at a speed so high that when he pulled out, he warped the fuselage of his fighter – the Mustang had to be scrapped after the mission. Two more P-51s were lost in the fray, with Lt Gene Browne surviving to be taken prisoner and Lt Wellington G Irving being killed. Oscar Hutton was also lost when his Mustang was hit by a drop tank jettisoned by another P-51.

On 19 July, 48 aircraft escorted the 49th BW's B-24s during their attack on Munich/Schleissheim airfield. Although four Bf 109s were spotted, they were too distant to be intercepted by the Mustangs.

The next day, the group was tasked with escorting the 47th, 55th and 304th BWs to Friedrichshafen, in Germany, followed by a fighter sweep northeast of the target. Once again, the Udine area provided good hunting, with a group of 20 enemy aircraft attacking the bombers from 'six o'clock low'. Several other groups, consisting of four aircraft each, held formation on either side of the bomber stream, apparently acting as decoys. The attacking fighters were set upon by the 332nd's Joseph Elsberry, Langdon Johnson, Armour McDaniel and Ed Toppins, who each destroyed an aircraft.

Wellington Irving was a flight leader on 18 July 1944, and his four Mustangs charged into a large group of enemy fighters to break up an attack on a group of bombers. The 'heavies' were not part of the 332nd FG's assigned bomb group, but the Mustang pilots found themselves well placed to intercept the enemy fighters when they missed their own rendezvous. In the melee that ensued, 'we must have spread those guys from here to Christmas in every direction', wrote Stanley Harris, who eluded four Fw 190s by diving away. Irving was not so lucky – he died when his aeroplane was shot down (*Lt Col Harold C Hayes Collection*)

While the Luftwaffe's interception proved fruitless, a ferocious flak barrage over the target destroyed three B-24s. The 332nd picked up two flak-damaged stragglers around Udine and escorted them to safety.

On 21 July the group sent 60 aircraft north to cover the withdrawal of the 5th BW from the Brux synthetic oil refinery, but weather prevented a rendezvous. The next day, the group provided escort for the 55th BW on yet another mission to Ploesti. Sixty P-51s shepherded the bombers, and while 16 to 20 German aircraft were spotted, they made no effort to attack so were ignored in return.

Coming off the target, Jimmy Walker and his flight dropped down to escort a damaged B-24, and were rewarded with a barrage of German flak for their efforts. All five Mustangs received varying degrees of damage, and Walker had to bail out of his crippled P-51C (42-103592) over eastern Serbia. Once on the ground, he ran into anti-communist partisans in the

A groundcrewman refills the all-important oxygen system bottles in the rear fuselage of a P-51C in July 1944 (*Jon Lake Collection*)

area, and they united Walker with nine other American airmen. His group was eventually rescued by a nighttime pick-up by a US aircraft following 39 days in occupied territory. Walker rejoined the 332nd in September.

INCREASED MISSION RATE

The pace of the escorts picked up as July drew to a close. On the 24th, 35 P-51s covered the 47th BW's B-24s in an attack on Genoa Harbour, and the following day 46 Mustangs watched over the 55th BW during a raid on the Herman Göring Tank Works at Linz, in Austria.

On the latter mission, the group's aeroplanes formed into three groups to cover the beginning, middle and end of the bomber formation. The Luftwaffe threw 40 Bf 109s at the 332nd's last two eight-ship groups, and this tactic resulted in the losses of Starling Penn and Alfred Carroll (both became PoWs). In return Capt Harold Sawyer downed an enemy fighter for his second confirmed kill, and damaged two more.

Due to this operational tempo, mechanical issues began to plague the group – on 26 July, 61 Mustangs took off, but 21 returned to base. This high abort rate was due in part to the group's newness to the P-51, but some of it could be explained by the skill level of the groundcrews. While many of the mechanics serving with regular squadrons had previous mechanical experience in civilian life, this was often not available to black enlisted men. Still, availability rates would gradually rise to equal those of other groups.

The 40 Mustangs that completed the mission to escort the 47th BW to Markendorf airfield in Austria on the 26th found enemy skies filled with German opposition. On the way to the target, the group sighted two groups of six Bf 109s, and another group of Fw 190s was seen near the target, but they remained out of range until the B-24s made their attack. At that point 18 Bf 109s attacked the 332nd, while ten more fighters remained above them as top cover, before finally splitting into two-aeroplane formations and diving on the bombers.

As usual, the German fighters tried to 'split-S' their way out of trouble, and as usual, the Mustangs made short work out of the fleeing aircraft,

Capt Ed Toppins sits in his P-51B *TOPPER III* prior to take-off at Ramitelli in 1944. The 99th retained the 'A' in the side markings applied to its Mustangs that the unit had originally introduced while flying P-40Ls in 1943 (*Herman Lawson via the National Museum of the USAF*)

with Ed Toppins scoring his fourth kill, William Green bagging one confirmed and one unconfirmed and Freddie Hutchins and Leonard Jackson scoring a single confirmed victory each. Weldon Groves shared a kill with a Mustang from another group, and Roger Romine and Luther Smith claimed unconfirmed victories. The group lost P-51B 42-4888 to the German fighters during the mission, although its pilot, Lt Charles Jackson, succeeded in evading capture and returned to the group on 28 August.

The good hunting continued the next day, when the escorts for a 47th BW raid on the Weiss armament works, near Budapest, were jumped by 25 Fw 190s and Bf 109s north of Lake Balaton. The latter attacked first, followed closely by the Fw 190s. One Mustang was sent down smoking in their initial pass, although the pilot was later safely returned to the squadron, and others were damaged, including Ed Gleed's P-51, which had two guns shot out.

Nevertheless, Gleed tenaciously stuck to the tail of a Bf 109 and began taking aim on it, while at the same time watching a second Bf 109 manoeuvring to get onto his tail. He eventually hit one of the ammunition magazines in his opponent's wing, blowing the latter off and sending the fighter hurtling earthwards. At almost the same time, the pursuing Messerschmitt was also shot down.

While Gleed and his flight climbed back up to escort the B-24s coming off the target, the bombers were attacked by a dozen Fw 190s, but these were in turn intercepted by the Mustangs and they broke off their attacks. As the German fighters tried to flee, the P-51 pilots gave chase, including Gleed in his two-gunned aircraft.

In the running battle which ensued, Gleed picked out an Fw 190 and followed it all the way down to the deck, before catching the aeroplane with a fatal burst. He had become separated from his wingman in the process and was now out of ammunition. Adding to his problems, Gleed was attacked by two more Fw 190s, which peppered his already damaged Mustang as he 'hedge-hopped' between hills in an effort to shake off his assailants. The chase streaked across a riverbed and between church steeples in a Hungarian town, and when Gleed spotted a valley that led in the general direction of Ramitelli, he pointed the Mustang towards home, firewalled the engine and left the two Fw 190s in his wake. Gleed eventually landed back at his base, where his engine almost immediately quit from fuel starvation.

While Gleed was fighting for his life, the rest of the 332nd FG had also been busy too. Alfred Gorham scored a double, and single kills were recorded by Claude Govan, Richard Hall, Leonard Jackson (his third) and Felix Kirkpatrick. This eight-kill haul had been accomplished without sacrificing the protection of the bombers, who once again lost no aircraft to enemy fighters.

Another mission to Ploesti on 28 July as escorts for the 55th BW saw 54 aircraft launch and 14 aborts. The group spied seven enemy aircraft in the target area but they were beyond interception range. One Bf 109 was spotted stalking two straggling 332nd P-51s, but the pilot of the Messerschmitt ran for home when the Mustangs broke into it.

After a day off, 43 Mustangs provided escort for the 5th BW's raid on the Tokol armament works in Budapest on the 30th. Prior to the group reaching the rendezvous point, an ANR Reggiane Re.2001 was spotted flying a parallel course to a straggling Mustang flown by 2Lt Carl Johnson. As his squadronmates radioed a warning to Johnson, the Re.2001 made a sharp turn and tried to hit his Mustang with a 90-degree deflection shot. Johnson pulled his P-51 inside the Reggiane and knocked it down with a few well-aimed bursts.

Later in the mission, a flight of 332nd aircraft spotted a single Bf 109 and gave chase. However, before they could open fire, a checkertailed Mustang (probably from the 325th FG) swooped in, forcing the red-tailed P-51s to take evasive action, and shot down the Bf 109.

On 31 July, it was the 47th BW's turn to hit Ploesti, and 65 Mustangs from the 332nd provided escort. The P-51s arrived at the rendezvous point on time, but had to wait five minutes for the bombers – the mission's only significant problem. One Bf 109 was spotted, but it was too far away to be attacked.

Two days later, 71 group aircraft launched (with 16 aborts) to escort the 5th BW to the Le Pousin oil storage facility and the Portes Les Valences railway marshalling yard in southern France. The group heard a report that 50 Bf 109s had been detected gathering around Toulon, but when the formation reached the city, no enemy aircraft were seen. On the way home, Lt Earl Sherrard was badly burned when he crash-landed his damaged Mustang, and he was eventually transferred out of the unit for treatment back in the USA.

The next day, 64 Mustangs were despatched as cover for 5th BW B-17s sent to bomb the Ober Raderach chemical works in Germany. A quartet of Bf 109s was spotted at 28,000 ft in the Udine area, but they made no attack on the bombers and failed to lure the escorting fighters away from their charges.

On 6 August the group was tasked with two missions. The first, launched at 0937 hrs, saw 64 Mustangs escorting the 55th BW to Avignon in support of the impending landings. No enemy aircraft were sighted. At 1510 hrs, Melvin Jackson led eight Mustangs that were tasked with escorting a B-25 that was returning to Italy after being forced to land in Yugoslavia.

Twenty-four hours later, it was back to Germany for the group – 69 Mustangs were launched, with 15 aborts, on an escort mission to the Blechammer oil refineries. The entirety of the German air resistance was a single Bf 109 that made one diving pass on the bomber formation, then streaked for the deck.

The routine of uneventful escorts was broken on 8 August during a mission that saw 53 Mustangs 'ride herd' on the 5th BW as it bombed the Gyer aircraft and car works in Hungary. When in the vicinity of Banja Luka, in Yugoslavia, Lt Alfonso Simmons was last seen heading away from the rest of the group into clouds. After he bailed out of his flak-damaged P-51C, Simmons joined up with a band of partisans and eventually returned to the group.

Two days later, 62 Mustangs escorted the 304th BW's B-24s to Ploesti to attack the Campina Stevea Romana oil refinery. No enemy aircraft were spotted during the mission. After almost ten days without directly confronting the Germans, the group was itching for more contact with the enemy. It would soon get more than its share.

ON THE DECK AND ABOVE THE CLOUDS

I n support of the coming Allied invasion of southern France, codenamed Operation *Dragoon*, the 332nd FG was ordered to conduct a series of ground attack sorties in addition to its seemingly endless schedule of bomber escort missions. And the first such operation it carried out, on 12 August, would prove costly.

The group was tasked with knocking out radar stations surrounding the harbour at Marseilles in advance of the invasion, and all four squadrons

The most successful fighting outfits within the USAAF in World War 2 all had one thing in common – a strong, well respected leader who flew with his pilots on virtually every mission. The 332nd FG was fortunate in having just such a man in Benjamin O Davis (*Jon Lake Collection*)

were assigned specific targets – these turned out to be well defended. The 99th FS attacked targets in Montpelier and Sete, destroying both stations. During his strafing run, recent arrival 2Lt Dick Macon had his fighter shot out from beneath him and he was forced to bail out at low altitude just before his Mustang crashed into a house. With a compound fracture of his shoulder and four broken vertebrae in his neck, Macon was quickly captured.

The 302nd FS strafed radar installations at Narbonne and Leucate, scoring hits on the primary targets and on nearby installations. As they bore in on the stations, the four-ship flight of Alton Ballard, Virgil Richardson, John Daniels and Alexander Jefferson encountered heavy flak at 15,000 ft. 'I looked back to find Jefferson and noticed that Daniels, who was flying in front of me, was going up in smoke', said Richardson – Daniels' Mustang pancaked into the harbour. Richardson pulled up and had just started following Ballard when Jefferson was also hit. Forced to bail out of his flaming Mustang, the latter pilot was quickly captured by the Germans and ended up in captivity with Macon and Daniels.

The 100th FS went after three targets around Marseilles and Cape Couronne, and all were believed to have been destroyed. The 301st FS, meanwhile, attacked four targets in the Toulon area, including a radar station. The antenna installations were seen to topple over under the weight of the squadron's fire, but flak claimed Lt Joseph Gordon and Langdon Johnson, both of whom were killed.

The following day, after first completing a 61-aeroplane escort for the 304th BW attack on the railway bridges at Avignon, the group was assigned yet another strafing mission. The 301st and 302nd FSs attacked the radar facilities around Cap Blanc, Camerat Capet and La Ciotat, while the 99th and 100th flew fighter sweeps of the Toulon area. Lt Luke Weathers and two of his fellow pilots from the 301st hit one radar installation and were rewarded by the sight of the antenna crumbling. The second flight overshot the target, so they strafed six small buildings nearby instead.

Rattle Snake of the 100th FS taxis out to the runway at Ramitelli prior to a mission, the fighter's crew chief sat on the wing guiding the pilot. The big nose of the Mustang meant that visibility from the cockpit was limited when the aircraft was on the ground (*National Museum of the USAF*)

Meanwhile, the 302nd's first flight attacked a six-centimetre wavelength-type antenna from deck level and observed hits and sparks from the target, then continued to fire on a nearby heavy machine gun position. Two aircraft were lost in the strafing mission, Lt Clarence Allen bailing out of his damaged machine over Elba. He was soon rescued, as was Robert O'Neil, who crash-landed on the beach near Toulon and was rescued by the Free French.

The nearby fighter sweep, meanwhile, became a strung-out affair, with one of the 100th's flights becoming lost. While they were trying to regain their bearings, two Bf 109s and two Fw 190s bounced them from 'five o'clock high'. The Mustangs turned into their attackers, and in the process of extricating themselves from the ambush, Lt George Rhodes found himself in position to fire several short 15- to 20-degree deflection shots at an Fw 190. The Focke-Wulf's left wing disintegrated and the aeroplane cartwheeled into the ground.

On 15 August the group was back at high altitude with the heavy bombers, 64 Mustangs escorting the 55th BW to Point St Esprit,

Looking the very picture of a fighter pilot, Louis Purnell leaves a briefing at Ramitelli. One of the original members of the 99th, Purnell took advantage of the advance field on the Yugoslavian island of Vis when his engine picked up a chunk of flak during the 17 August 1944 mission to Ploesti (*National Museum of the USAF*)

Douzare, Le Teil, Bourg and St Andeal, in southern France. Two enemy fighters were observed, but they were too far away to be intercepted. Lt Wilson Eagleson's fighter was hit in the engine by flak and started losing coolant, but he stayed with the Mustang until the Merlin froze up and then he bailed out. By then he was over Allied territory, and a squad of American troops saw him jump. By the time Eagleson had walked the half-mile to a nearby road, the soldiers were waiting for him in a Jeep to provide him with a lift back to Ramitelli!

The next day, during a bomber escort mission for the 55th BW to the Ober Raderach chemical works in Germany, another pilot was forced to jump. 1Lt Herbert V Clark of the 99th FS, who was one of the unit's flight leaders, was shot down by flak. He evaded capture and ended up commanding a band of partisans conducting raids against the Germans in northern Italy. Clark was reunited with the group eight months later on 7 May 1945, just as the war ended.

On 17 August, 55 Mustangs escorted the 304th BW on a mission to Ploesti. Two aircraft, including the Mustang of Louis Purnell, were damaged by flak and landed on the island of Vis, off the coast of Yugoslavia, where an emergency strip had been established.

Two days later, 50 P-51s escorted the 47th BW on yet another Ploesti mission. One Mustang was lost when Lt William Thomas crash-landed his aeroplane on Pisnosa Island 20 minutes after taking off. Thomas was returned to the group by the air-sea rescue boat.

20 August provided evidence of both the 332nd's growing reputation and of the declining aggressiveness of the enemy. A fleet of 59 Mustangs escorted the 5th BW on a raid on the oil refineries at Oswiecim, in Poland. The group was menaced by 18 Bf 109s and Fw 190s that lined up to attack the last P-51 flight, but when the four Mustangs turned into them the German fighters scattered and ran.

Following a day off, Capt Erwin Lawrence led 52 Mustangs aloft to shepherd the 55th BW to the Kornenburg oil refinery in Vienna on the 21st. The bombers were 18 minutes late to the rendezvous point, so Lawrence ordered the group to orbit until they arrived. During the escort, 20 Bf 109s were spotted near Lake Balaton, and three more at a higher altitude made a move towards the bomber formations, but they were chased off by a flight of Mustangs.

The closest the group came to actual combat was when a solitary Spitfire stumbled across the combined formation in the target area and made the mistake of pointing its nose at the bombers. A flight of Mustangs made one firing pass before the unharmed Spitfire waggled its wings and sped away.

That same day, 18 Mustangs escorted six C-47s to Yugoslavia on an afternoon mission to drop supplies to the local Partisans. The mission was uneventful and all the aircraft returned safely.

On 22 August, a 60-Mustang formation guarded the 55th BW during an attack on Markersdorf airfield, in Germany. Over the target, the bombers were set upon by 14 Bf 109s. Seven were seen to enter a Lufbery Circle, then dive through the bomber formation with no apparent success. Lts William Hill and Luke Weathers tagged onto the tail of one of the Bf 109s and, from 250 yards, fired from 24,000 ft all the way down to the deck. Whether or not their claim would be verified had to wait, but after

Charles McGee, shown with his Mustang *"KITTEN"*, knocked down an Fw 190 on 24 August 1944 while returning from a sweep to Pardubice. McGee eventually amassed 408 combat missions, flying Mustangs in Korea and RF-4 Phantom IIs over Vietnam – the highest tally for any US airman (*Charles McGee*)

their gun camera film was developed, each was credited with half of a confirmed kill on 28 August.

SCREENING AIRFIELD ATTACKS

Screening heavy bomber attacks on Axis airfields seemed to be the best way to scare up fighter opposition in August. On the 24th, 52 P-51s escorted the 5th BW to Pardubice airfield, in Czechoslovakia, and although the escort to the target proved uneventful, on the way home a Bf 109 attacked Lt John Briggs' flight from 'six o'clock'. The Mustangs turned sharply into their attacker, and Briggs positioned himself behind and below the now-fleeing and climbing fighter, firing bursts from 250 yards at a height of 24,000 ft. Seeing no results, he pressed as close as 25 yards and opened fire again at 35,000 ft. Pieces of the Bf 109 flew back toward Briggs, followed shortly by the pilot, who bailed out.

Meanwhile, Lt Charles McGee had spotted an Fw 190 flying 180 degrees to his course, so he peeled off to attack. The German pilot saw the red-tailed Mustang and abruptly headed for the deck, using a series of evasive manoeuvres to try to shake off McGee before finally resorting to a steep dive towards the airfield at Pardubice. 'I recall as we flashed over the

field proper in a right turn, there was a hangar and several aircraft fires brightly blazing', McGee said. He manoeuvred in behind the Fw 190 and fired a burst that he suspected hit the aircraft's control cables, because the German fighter made two erratic turns and slammed into the ground. McGee's wingman, Roger Romine, saw the aeroplane crash and confirmed the victory.

Although he had got his kill, McGee was now in trouble, as the airfield's anti-aircraft guns were all trained on him. 'I made a low-altitude dash out of the area to avoid ground fire', he recalled, and for good measure, he 'got a good burst off on a locomotive at a railroad stop', before climbing to rejoin the group.

About five minutes later, at 1235 hrs, Lt William Thomas spied another Fw 190 at 24,000 ft at about the same time that the German pilot spotted him. Instead of turning into Thomas, he tried to dive to safety, but the Mustang pilot caught up to him at an altitude of about 800 ft and fired six times at him from 75-100 yards. Thomas' final burst was a 30-degree deflection shot, which caused the Fw 190 to hit the ground and crumple up into a tangle of smoking wreckage.

On 25 August, 60 Mustangs returned to Czechoslovakian skies when they escorted the B-17s of the 5th BW sent to attack Brno airfield. The mission went exactly as briefed, but this time no enemy aircraft rose to challenge the bombers, and all the 332nd's P-51s were back at Ramitelli by 1315 hrs.

The next day, 56 P-51s accompanied the 304th BW to attack barracks near the Bulgarian airfield at Banasea. The bombers were ten minutes late

On occasion, Ramitelli was used as an emergency strip for Fifteenth Air Force bombers, although its narrow taxiways presented exhausted pilots with an exercise in precision ground handling. Here, men of the 332nd pose next to their latest visitor (*Western Aerospace Museum*)

Capt Wendell O Pruitt leaves a treasured ring with his crew chief, SSgt Samuel W Jacobs, prior to flying his next mission. Pruitt destroyed five aeroplanes on the ground during the 332nd's strafing attacks on the airfields at Prostejou and Kostoleo on 27 August 1944 (*National Museum of the USAF*)

arriving at the rendezvous point, and when they did eventually attempt to hit their target, the Mustang pilots saw that their ordnance had fallen harmlessly in some nearby woods. Worse still, 2Lt Henry Wise of the 99th FS was forced to bail out when his oil pressure dropped and his Merlin started to smoke heavily.

Taken prisoner in Bulgaria, Wise's fortunes changed dramatically when his captors severed their ties with Germany. While the latter marched a number of PoWs out of Bulgaria, Wise and hundreds of others were left behind. They were eventually evacuated through Turkey and Egypt, and before finally making it back to Italy, where Wise returned to the group in

September. He was immediately promoted to first lieutenant and issued with orders sending him home.

On 27 August, the 57 Mustangs sent to escort the 55th and 304th BWs to Blechammer, in Germany, had completed their rendezvous and escort when Melvin Jackson spotted a single German aircraft taking off from an airfield near Prostejou, in Czechoslovakia. The group dropped down and attacked this site, along with an airfield at nearby Kostoleo. A lack of flak allowed the 332nd to strafe a large number of aircraft, and by the time the pilots had exhausted their ammunition, 13 Ju 52/3ms, four Ju 87s and three He 111s had been destroyed and four Ju 87s, four He 111s, nine Ju 52/3ms and an Me 323 Gigant had been damaged.

The chief contributors to German misery this day were Wendell Pruitt, who destroyed three Stukas and two He 111s, Spann Watson, who accounted for four Ju 52/3ms and an He 111, and Luther Smith, who destroyed three Ju 52/3ms and an He 111. For good measure, the group also strafed the aerodrome's barracks and an unlucky locomotive that happened to be near the airfield. The 332nd suffered no casualties.

Four dozen P-51s covered the 47th BW's raid on the Miskolc main railway marshalling yard, in Yugoslavia, on 28 August. All returned safely to base. The following day, 55 Mustangs escorted the 5th BW's attack on the Bohumin and Privoser oil refineries and the Morvaska main railway marshalling yard. Lt Emile Clifton developed engine trouble during the mission and bailed out of his Mustang over Yugoslavia, although he returned to the group a month later.

CARNAGE AT GROSSWARDEIN

If the Luftwaffe refused to come up, the 332nd was happy to come down, and on 30 August the group found about 150 aircraft at Grosswardein airfield, in Rumania, camouflaged rather poorly under stacks of hay. Despite moderate flak, the 302nd FS made seven passes, the 100th five passes and the 99th three passes. After several attack runs, the biggest hazard facing the Mustang pilots was the rising smoke from burning aircraft – the entire field was blanketed with an oily haze caused by flaming hay and petrol.

The kills were distributed among 46 different pilots, with Roger Romine of the 302nd destroying seven aircraft and Alfonso Davis and Freddie Hutchins four apiece. The collection of destroyed aircraft reads like an inventory of German wartime aviation – 30 Ju 88s, 12 He 111s, seven Fw 189s, six Ju 87s, six Do 217s, five Ju 52/3ms, four Fw 190s, three Bf 109s, three Go 242 gliders, two Me 323s, two Me 210s, two Bf 110s and a single Ar 96. In all, the group destroyed 83 aircraft and damaged 31 more, making this the most destructive day in the 332nd's history.

'Spanky' Roberts served as commander of the group in Col Davis' absence, and he was assistant group commander when the colonel was in Italy. During the 30 August massacre at Grosswardein airfield, Roberts destroyed two Ju 88s and damaged a Ju 87 (*Western Aerospace Museum*)

Capt Andrew 'Jug' Turner, CO of the 100th FS, hams it up for the camera while sitting in his Mustang *Skipper's Darlin' III*. Turner, a steady and respected leader, later served as deputy group commander of the post-war 332nd (*National Museum of the USAF*)

Adding to the carnage, a single Mustang destroyed four tank cars on a nearby siding. The only casualty was Lt Charles Williams, who was shot down in the target area and taken prisoner.

Escort missions resumed on 31 August, when the 100th and 301st sent 32 Mustangs to shepherd second-wave B-17s in an attack on Popesti airfield. A similar mission was given to the 99th and 302nd FSs, which sent 31 fighters to cover the third wave of bombers. No enemy air activity was observed. The following day, the group again provided escort for B-17s attacking this airfield, but weather and poor navigation prevented the 301st and 302nd from completing the mission.

On 2 September, 61 Mustangs conducted an armed reconnaissance of the road between Stalac, Cuprija and Osipaonica, in Serbia. During the mission, the group strafed goods wagons at the train station at Krusevac and damaged a nearby truck – two aircraft attacked five wagons on a siding and scored hits on all of them. Later, a single unnamed pilot, who had taken off late and was hurrying to join the group, spotted a 30-truck convoy and raked it from end to end, setting three vehicles on fire and damaging ten more.

In an effort to prevent the Germans from shifting troops into northern Europe to repel the Allied advance, the Fifteenth Air Force turned its attentions to the destruction of railway bridges in northern Italy and Hungary. Some 59 P-51s were tasked with covering the 304th BW's attack on the Hungarian bridges at Szolnok and Szeged on 3 September, while Capt Erwin Lawrence led an escort of 45 P-51s for the 304th BW's bridge-busting mission to Tagliamento Casarsa and Latisana, in Italy, the following day. A similar mission on 5 September was flown by the 5th

Capt William Mattison's crew chief helps him strap into his Mustang before a mission. Mattison led the 8 September 1944 mission to Ilandza, in Yugoslavia, during which 18 German aeroplanes were destroyed on the ground (*Western Aerospace Museum*)

BW, with Andrew 'Jug' Turner leading the 54 Mustangs sent aloft. All three missions saw no German air opposition.

For a change of pace, the 5th BW attacked the main railway marshalling yard at Oradea, in Rumania, on 6 September. The 332nd sent 63 Mustangs as escort, and again there was no opposition.

Two days later, Capt William Mattison led 42 aircraft to the Luftwaffe airfield at Ilandza, in Yugoslavia. About 20 aeroplanes were spotted, and 23 Mustangs dropped down to the deck to strafe them, covered by 14 others. The attack destroyed 18 aircraft, including five Ju 52/3ms, four Ju 88s, three Do 217s, three Fw 200s and a single Fw 190, Bf 109 and He 111. The Mustang flown by Lt James A Calhoun was hit by flak, and while his fellow pilots thought that he had deliberately crash-landed his fighter in the target area, Calhoun was killed. The group then continued on to the airfield at Alibunar, where 15 P-51s attacked parked aircraft while 26 fighters flew top cover in expectation that the now-alerted Luftwaffe would respond. Instead, the group eliminated 15 Fw 190s, two Bf 109s and an SM.84 transport in the face of moderate flak. For good measure, the 332nd also destroyed a locomotive on its way home.

On 10 September, the 332nd assembled at Ramitelli for a particularly meaningful ceremony. Gen Benjamin O Davis Snr was on hand to award the DFC to his son, Col Benjamin O Davis Jr, as well as Capt Joseph Elsberry and 1Lts Jack Holsclaw and Clarence 'Lucky' Lester.

Gen Benjamin O Davis Snr pins the DFC on his son, Col Benjamin O Davis Jnr. At one time, these two men were the only black non-chaplain officers in the entire US Army. Lined up to Davis Jnr's left are Joseph Elsberry, Jack Holsclaw and Clarence Lester, who also received the award at the 10 September 1944 ceremony (*National Museum of the USAF*)

After 48 hours off, the group sent 71 Mustangs out at 1039 hrs as escorts for the 5th BW – four spares turned for home at 1220 hrs. On their way back to Ramitelli, two of the latter pilots sighted a twin-engined aircraft in the landing pattern at Udine South airfield and they dropped down to check it out. After the tower fired two red flares, the aeroplane disappeared into the haze.

The two red-tailed Mustangs were already at low altitude, and they spotted ten aircraft hiding in sandbag revetments under camouflage netting near the base perimeter. The Mustangs circled to the right and made a solitary pass, damaging one single-engined and three twin-engined aeroplanes, before a small-calibre anti-aircraft shell hit one of the fighters in the rudder, forcing them to abandon the attack.

On 13 September, 57 P-51s escorted the 304th BW to the Blechammer North oil refinery. Although three German fighters were spotted in the distance, they did not attack the bombers. During the mission, 2Lt Wilbur F Long went missing, his fellow pilots assuming that he had crash-landed P-51C 42-103925. Long was quickly captured by the Germans and spent the rest of the war in Stalag Luft VIIA.

Budapest was the target on 17 and 18 September, 63 Mustangs escorting the 5th BW strike on the Rakos railway marshalling yards during the first raid. While the bombers were on their run, a single twin-engined aircraft was spotted speeding over the city. The bogie was identified as an RAF Mosquito, which flew through the target area unmolested. The next day, the 304th BW attacked Budapest's Shell oil refinery and railway bridges whilst under the protection of 51 332nd Mustangs. Once again a single Mosquito was observed flying over the target area during the B-17s' bomb run.

On 20 September, 65 Mustangs escorted B-24s from the 304th BW sent to pound Malacky airfield, in Czechoslovakia. There was no aerial opposition. The next day, 62 Mustangs were sent out as an escort for the 5th BW's attack on the Debreczen railway marshalling yards in Hungary, but weather delayed the fighters by 18 minutes and the bombers were ahead of schedule by ten minutes, ruining any chance of a rendezvous. The last two bomb groups were dropping their bombs just as the 332nd arrived over the target area. However, the Luftwaffe was unable to take advantage of the situation – again, no German aircraft were seen anywhere near the 'heavies'.

Two days later, another mission was completed in which the USAAF went unmolested by enemy aircraft, although while escorting B-17s away from a target in the Munich area, Chris Newman's Mustang *Goodwiggle* was hit by flak. He had nursed the crippled fighter as far as the Adriatic when his engine burst into flames and he was forced to bail out. Newman was quickly rescued by the efficient air-sea rescue service and returned to the group.

2Lt Leonard Willette was not so lucky, for about ten miles north of Lake Chiem, in Germany, he radioed that he was losing oil pressure and would be forced to bail out. Willette was declared killed in action in January 1945.

On 23 September, 50 Mustangs accompanied the 5th BW's mission to destroy a synthetic oil plant in Germany. There was no air opposition. The following day saw another milk run, with 37 P-51s accompanying the 304th BW to Athens airfield. Although the local flak batteries were assisted by four warships offshore, all aircraft returned to base.

The missions were now becoming almost routine, with no enemy aircraft sighted for almost two weeks, and the intensity of combat having steadily slackened. This situation would be swiftly reversed in the coming month.

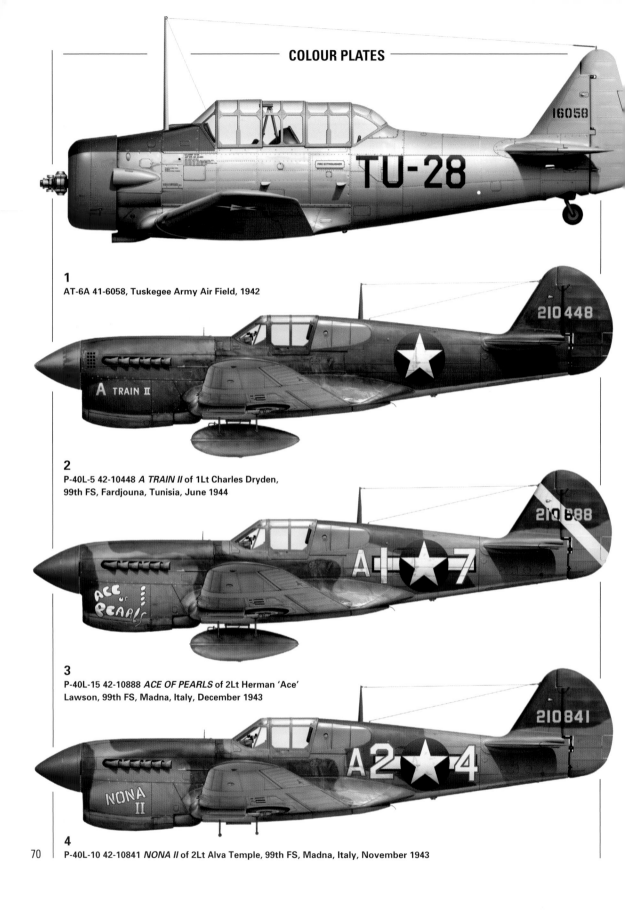

1
AT-6A 41-6058, Tuskegee Army Air Field, 1942

2
P-40L-5 42-10448 *A TRAIN II* of 1Lt Charles Dryden,
99th FS, Fardjouna, Tunisia, June 1944

3
P-40L-15 42-10888 *ACE OF PEARLS* of 2Lt Herman 'Ace'
Lawson, 99th FS, Madna, Italy, December 1943

4
P-40L-10 42-10841 *NONA II* of 2Lt Alva Temple, 99th FS, Madna, Italy, November 1943

5
P-40L-15 42-10461 *JOSEPHINE* of 1Lt Charles Bailey, 99th FS, Madna, Italy, January 1944

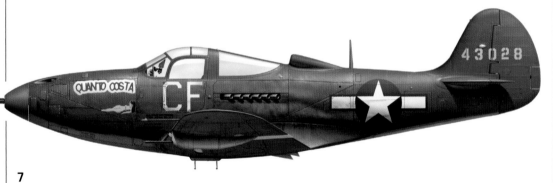

6
P-40L-15 42-10855 of 1Lt Robert W Diez, 99th FS, Madna, Italy, January 1944

7
P-39Q-20 44-3028 *QUANTO COSTA* of 1Lt Samuel Curtis, 100th FS, Capodichino, Italy, May 1944

8
P-47D (serial unknown) of 1Lt Gwynne Peirson, Ramitelli, 302nd FS, Italy, June 1944

9
P-47D-16 42-75971 of 2Lt Lloyd Hathcock, 301st FS, Ramitelli, Italy, May 1944

10
P-47D-22 (serial, pilot and unit unknown), Ramitelli, Italy, June 1944

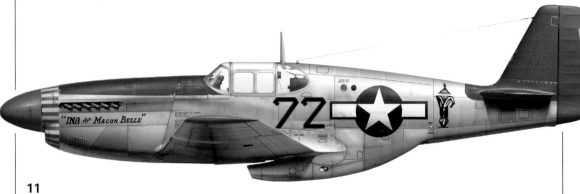

11
P-51C-10 (serial unknown) *"INA THE MACON BELLE"* of Lt Lee Archer Jnr, 302nd FS, Ramitelli, Italy, July 1944

12
P-51C (serial unknown) *Joedebelle* of Capt Joseph Elsberry, 301st FS, Ramitelli, Italy, July 1944

13
P-51B/C (serial unknown) *TOPPER III* of Capt Edward Toppins, 99th FS, Ramitelli, Italy, August 1944

14
P-51B/C (serial unknown) *ALICE-JO* of Capt Wendell Pruitt, 302nd FS, Ramitelli, Italy, September 1944

15
P-51C-10 42-103960 *Skipper's Darlin' III* of Capt Andrew 'Jug' Turner, Ramitelli, Italy, September 1944

16
P-51C-10 42-103956 *Miss-Pelt* of 1Lt Clarence 'Lucky' Lester, 100th FS, Ramitelli, Italy, September 1944

17
P-51C (serial unknown) *APACHE II* of 1Lt Henry Perry, 99th FS, Ramitelli, Italy, September 1944

18
P-51C (serial unknown) *LUCIFER* of 1Lt Luther Smith, 302nd FS, Ramitelli, Italy, October 1944

19
P-51D (serial unknown) *"Little Freddie"* of 1Lt Freddie Hutchins, 302nd FS, Ramitelli, Italy, October 1944

20
P-51C (serial unknown) *DAISEY MAE of* Capt Woody Crockett, 100th FS, Ramitelli, Italy, November 1944

21
P-51C (serial unknown) *By Request* of Col Benjamin O Davis, CO of the 332nd FG, Ramitelli, Italy, December 1944

22
P-51C (serial unknown) *MY BUDDY* of Capt Charles Bailey, 99th FS, Ramitelli, Italy, December 1944

23
P-51D-15 44-15648 *LOLLIPOOP II* of 1Lt Spurgeon Ellington, 100th FS, Ramitelli, Italy, December 1944

24
P-51D (serial unknown) *Creamer's Dream* of 1Lt Charles White, 301st FS, Ramitelli, Italy, January 1945

25
P-51D-15 44-15648 *DUCHESS ARLENE* of 1Lt Robert W Williams, 301st FS, Ramitelli, Italy, March 1945

26
P-51D (serial unknown) *TALL in the SADDLE* of 1Lt George Hardy, 99th FS, Ramitelli, Italy, February 1945

27
P-51B (serial unknown) *KITTEN* of 2Lt Leon 'Woodie' Spears, 302nd FS, Ramitelli, Italy, March 1945

28
P-51D (serial unknown) *MEATBALL RAP II* of Flt Off Charles Lane, 99th FS, Ramitelli, Italy, March 1945

1
332nd Fighter Group

2
99th Fighter Squadron

3
100th Fighter Squadron

4
301st Fighter Squadron

5
302nd Fighter Squadron

THE TOUGHEST MONTH

On the morning of 4 October 1944, a flight of four Mustangs escorted three C-47s to Sofia, orbited while they landed and shepherded them back to safety. It was an uneventful start to what would duly become a bloody day, and the start of the 332nd FG's bloodiest month in combat.

At 1058 hrs, 37 Mustangs took off under the command of Erwin Lawrence, CO of the 99th FS, to strafe the Greek airfields at Tatoi, Kalamaki and Eleusis. At the assigned point, the 99th, 100th and 301st split off to attack the three target airfields. The pilots of the 99th strafed Tatoi from deck level, spotting 25 to 30 well-dispersed enemy aeroplanes as they ran in.

Closing on the target, Lawrence, who was leading his final mission before rotating home, suddenly rolled over at low altitude in his fighter and crashed in flames. Squadronmates believed that he had struck a cable strung across the airfield as a crude form of air defence. 2Lt Kenneth I Williams also crashed in the target area, but he survived and was taken prisoner. 'Four fires were seen on the aerodrome during the initial pass, but two of the fires are believed to have been from our own

Howard Baugh, 'Spanky' Roberts and Erwin Lawrence pose with one of the group's Mustangs in the summer of 1944. Lawrence, who took over as CO of the 99th in April 1944, flew almost 100 missions and scored a kill over Anzio in a P-40L. A popular leader, he was killed on 4 October 1944 when his Mustang struck a cable while strafing the airfield at Tatoi, in Greece (*National Museum of the USAF*)

Henry 'Herky' Perry strikes a jaunty pose next to his Mustang, *APACHE II*, in Italy. On 6 October 1944 Perry destroyed a Ju 52/3m and damaged two more twin-engined aircraft during a strafing attack at Tatoi (*Herman Lawson via the National Museum of the USAF*)

aeroplanes lost in the target area', Ray Ware wrote in his mission report. Almost all the German aircraft on the airfield were damaged, with Herman Lawson claiming a Ju 52/3m destroyed – small reward for the loss of a popular commander.

The 100th FS attacked Kalamaki airfield at much the same time, destroying three aeroplanes and damaging eight more. Meanwhile, the 301st strafed the base at Eleusis, destroying four Ju 52/3ms and an SM.79.

While the other three squadrons were strafing in Greece, the 302nd FS was assigned the job of escorting 12 C-47s to Bucharest – 14 Mustangs completed this uneventful mission.

The Greek airfields at Tatoi, Kalamaki and Eleusis, plus the strip at Megara, were once again the target on 6 October, and this time the group was led by Col Davis. Soon after departing Ramitelli, Lt Elbert Hudson's sputtering Mustang belly-landed on the forward airfield at Biferano. It was a bad omen.

Andrew Marshall is debriefed after his return to the group on 18 October 1944. He was able to evade capture after his Mustang was shot out from under him during the 6 October mission against the airfield at Eleusis. Marshall's luck held until 29 December 1944, when he was killed in action during a bomber escort mission to Passau (*Western Aerospace Museum*)

The 99th struck Tatoi, destroying two Ju 52/3ms, an Fw 200 and an He 111. The 100th again attacked Kalamaki, where George Rhodes destroyed an He 111. Two other German aircraft were damaged on the airfield, but during the attack 1Lt Carroll S Woods' P-51 was hit by flak and, with its tail on fire, crashed on the aerodrome. The pilot would spend the rest of the war in Stalag Luft VIIA.

At Eleusis, the 301st arrived to find that the Germans had evacuated all their aircraft except for one derelict Ju 52/3m. Even so, the squadron shot up the base and set a fuel dump on fire. In the process, however, 2Lt Andrew D Marshall's fighter was hit by flak and he was eventually forced to bail out – Marshall would return to the group with slight injuries on 18 October. 2Lt Joe A Lewis, a veteran of 51 missions, was not so lucky. His aircraft was last seen trailing smoke on its way out of the target area, and after his Mustang went down, he joined Carroll Woods in captivity.

The 302nd found Megara similarly empty, but worked it over just the same. 1Lt Freddie Hutchins opened fire on what turned out to be an ammunition dump, and as the target exploded violently, his Mustang, *Little Freddie*, was raked with flak that blew off its right wing tip and shredded its tail. Hutchins could hear small arms fire rattling against the aeroplane, and he pressed himself down against the armour plate, only to

The spartan conditions at Ramitelli are evident in this view of the 100th FS Mustangs at rest in their gravel 'revetments'. Virtually all maintenance on the group's aircraft was performed in the open, often in the extremes of the Italian weather (*National Museum of the USAF*)

Group flight surgeon Vance Marchbanks kept a close watch on the group's pilots in light of the large numbers of missions they were required to fly. When he sensed men needed a break, they were sent to a recreation centre in nearby Naples, where this photograph was snapped. Pictured (from left to right) are Lt Wylie Selden, Capt Freddie Hutchins, an unnamed Red Cross volunteer and Lts George Gray and F Johnson (*Western Aerospace Museum*)

have a burst come through the bottom of the cockpit and pepper his legs with fragments.

Now in agony, Hutchins nursed the Mustang to a spot three miles west of Megara and crash-landed whilst still travelling at 250 mph. Knocked unconscious, he eventually awoke to find that he was still strapped into the cockpit of his fighter, but that its engine was now several hundred feet away and the wings and tail had been ripped off. His goggles were smashed against his forehead and his legs hurt terribly. Greek civilians rushed to the site and lifted Hutchins out of the cockpit, placing him on the back of a donkey and leading it to the home of a doctor. The doctor rubbed him with olive oil and bandaged his wounds, before putting him to bed. Hutchins awoke after being bitten by dozens of fleas, and the itchy pilot decided to make it back to friendly forces under his own steam. Managing to avoid capture, he returned to the group on 23 October.

Despite losing five Mustangs the day before, 53 P-51s under the command of 'Spanky' Roberts escorted the 5th BW to the Lobau oil refinery in Vienna on 7 October. During the outbound leg, 1Lt Robert Wiggins survived the crash-landing of his Mustang at Vis, but Flt Off Carl J Woods and 2Lt Roosevelt Stiger went missing and were never heard from again. Fuel became a major issue during this mission, with the 23 pilots that were forced to land at forward fields having to be collected by a fleet of trucks.

After a three-day break to rest and re-equip, the group was sent out on an interdiction mission from Budapest to Bratislava, in Czechoslovakia,

Amid the losses came Lee 'Buddy' Archer's three-kill day over Kaposvas airfield, in Hungary, on 11 October 1944. One of these victories was classified as a shared kill for many years because the aircraft had possibly been damaged by Freddie Hutchins before Archer downed it. The latter was duly given sole credit for the victory during a review of claims conducted by the USAF in the early 1990s, thus boosting Archer's tally of aerial successes to five. He duly became the 332nd FG's only ace of World War 2 (*National Museum of the USAF*)

John F Briggs congratulates Wendell O Pruitt at the end of the latter's combat tour. The second half of the 'Gruesome Twosome' with Archer, Pruitt scored three kills. His two victories in the Mustang came during the 11 October 1944 mission, and it could have been three kills had the guns of his P-51B not jammed in the middle of the engagement (*National Museum of the USAF*)

in an effort to cut off German troops retreating from the Eastern Front. Weather prevented all but 20 of the 72 Mustangs that set out from finding targets, but those who managed to penetrate holes in the cloud at Esztergom, on the Danube River in Hungary, were rewarded with the destruction of 17 enemy aircraft at three airfields. The Mustang pilots also wrecked two locomotives, an oil wagon and a fuel dump, whilst six barges, a locomotive and a goods wagon were damaged.

Lt George Gray of the 99th destroyed two Me 210s, an He 111 and a biplane trainer on the ground during this mission, while Lt Richard S Harder also claimed a pair of Me 210s and an He 111. The only thing that marred the day was George Rhodes' forced-landing at Ramitelli, which wrote off the Mustang but left the pilot safe.

On 11 October, 63 Mustangs set out again for the area between Budapest and Bratislava. While on patrol over enemy territory, the 99th FS sent 14 aircraft down to investigate a report of a biplane overhead Kaposvas airfield. Although 35 to 40 aircraft were seen parked in or near revetments, no biplane could be found. Nevertheless, the 99th attacked the aerodrome just the same. The first pass was made from east to west, with each of the nine subsequent passes being flown in a counter-clockwise manner.

The attack left 18 aeroplanes burning, including four Bf 109s, five He 111s, five Ju 88s, an Fw 200, an Fw 190, an unidentified trainer and an unidentified twin-engined aircraft. Five other aeroplanes were damaged. Lt George Gray bagged five on the ground, while Lt Hannibal Cox ignited three others.

The 302nd also received a radio report that an enemy aircraft – this time an He 111 – had been spotted near another landing field. As Capt Wendell Pruitt's flight was looking for the Heinkel, Lee Archer spotted a group of enemy aircraft climbing at 'two o'clock low'. Pruitt gave the order to attack, but before his flight could peel off, it was jumped by nine Bf 109s that were covering two He 111s.

'Two Messerschmitts were flying abreast', Archer reported. 'I tore the wing off one with a long burst. The other one slid in behind Pruitt. I pulled up, zeroed in, hit the gun button and watched him explode'. Pruitt, who had already bagged an He 111 and a Bf 109 by this point, was

Armour McDaniel succeeded in destroying one of the three oil barges sunk on 11 October, but the exploding barge sent a shower of jagged debris into the air which peppered McDaniel's Mustang. Amazed that his fighter had held together, the pilot surveys the damage with his groundcrew (*National Museum of the USAF*)

giving chase to another Messerschmitt fighter when his guns jammed. Archer took up the chase, following the fleeing fighter to the deck. 'He appeared to be trying to land', the Mustang pilot recalled. 'I opened up at ground level, hit him with a long volley and he crashed.' Flak and small arms fire in turn drove Archer back to higher altitude. He would conclude his three-kill day with a landing on the island of Vis, during which his aircraft ran off the perforated steel planking runway and damaged the propeller.

In just 15 minutes, all three He 111s and six of the nine Bf 109s had been destroyed, with Milton Brooks, William Green, Roger Romine and Luther Smith downing the four enemy aircraft not accounted for by 'the Gruesome Twosome'. The fight had raged from 7000 ft all the way down to the deck, and pilots reported that the Germans used very poor and, in some instances, no evasive tactics. After countering the enemy fighters, the 302nd turned its attentions to the nearby airfield, destroying three He 111s, two Bf 109s, a Ju 88, a Bf 110 and an unidentified biplane trainer. Four more aircraft were damaged.

The 100th and 301st FSs continued on towards their assigned targets, only to be disrupted by several yellow-tailed Mustangs (probably from the 52nd FG), which turned into them as if to attack. The 100th was sent to counter the P-51s, and fortunately the two sides avoided any acts of fratricide. Once the 'threat' from their fellow Mustangs had gone, the 100th strafed a railway siding and a factory, damaging three locomotives, three passenger carriages, 30 goods wagons, 25 trucks on the nearby highway and the factory itself, which was surrounded by three parking lots filled with an additional 45 trucks.

While the 100th strafed the factory and railway line, the 301st set its sights on 50 oil barges in the Danube. Three were sent to the bottom and a further 11 were shot up during the attack by 18 Mustangs. 1Lt Walter L McCreary was hit by flak whilst making his strafing run, and he was forced to bail out of his stricken P-51 over Kaspovar, in Hungary. McCreary would spend the remainder of the war at Stalags Luft III and IVA.

On 13 October, after the primary task of escorting the 304th BW to the Blechammer oil refineries had been completed, the group's 60 Mustangs dropped down to replicate the previous day's strafing successes. A four-ship flight from the 99th attacked a train headed east from Bratislava, damaging two locomotives and a flat car loaded with trucks. Three of the 100th's Mustangs also shot up six previously-damaged goods wagons, while four other P-51s from the 302nd strafed a train, destroying a locomotive and damaging goods wagons and coal cars. They also strafed a small house alongside the track, and this exploded so violently that it was undoubtedly being used to store ammunition.

Two flights from the 302nd swooped in on Tapolcza airfield, destroying seven aeroplanes, including three He 111s and two Ju 52/3ms – six more aircraft were damaged. The mission proved costly, however, as two Mustangs were shot down by intense flak. 1Lt Walter Westmoreland, in P-51C 43-24905, was killed, and 1Lt William Green, in P-51C 44-10943, parachuted into a field near Sisak and returned to the group after spending a week with Tito's partisans in Yugoslavia.

A short while later 1Lt Luther Smith's P-51B (43-24894) caught fire over Hungary after suffering damage from an exploding ammunition dump. He rolled the fighter over in order to bail out, but the aeroplane snapped into an inverted flat spin, snagging Smith half-in and half-out of the cockpit. He tried to clamber back in to free himself, but jammed his right foot between the rudder pedals and the floor. At that point, the slipstream tore off Smith's oxygen mask and he passed out, but somehow he was thrown free of the Mustang and his parachute deployed. When he came to, he was suspended in a tree, his right foot and hip badly broken.

Alfonso Davis had been a cavalry trooper at Fort Leavenworth, in Kentucky, before being accepted into flight school. Davis replaced Mac Ross as group operations officer, then became commander of the 99th FS upon the death of Erwin Lawrence. Davis himself was lost on 29 October when, without a word, his aircraft simply pulled out of formation and plunged to earth (*National Museum of the USAF*)

Smith spent time in a series of German hospitals, suffering from bone infections and dysentery, before being sent to Stalag Luft VIIA. When he was finally liberated, he weighed just 70 lbs.

On the morning of 14 October, 52 aircraft left Ramitelli to escort the 49th BW's B-24s to the Odertal oil refineries in Germany. The Luftwaffe offered no opposition, but losses continued just the same, as Lt Rual Bell of the 100th FS suffered mechanical problems an hour from the target and bailed out of his P-51C. He returned to the squadron in December.

After Bell's bail out, the group received a much needed respite from the losses. On 16 October, Col Davis led an escort for 5th BW bombers sent to attack the Brux oil refineries, and although no aerial opposition was met, one Mustang was holed by flak. The next day, three P-51s accompanied a single B-17 to Bucharest at 0720 hrs, followed by a 51-aeroplane mission escorting the 5th BW to the Blechammer South oil refinery. The only other aircraft spotted during the mission was a lone Mosquito south of Brno.

On the 20th, a second 51-aeroplane mission to escort the 5th BW to the Brux oil refineries again met with no resistance. The only aircraft spotted this time were B-26s near Venice. Later in the day, two Mustangs escorted an OA-10 Catalina to rescue seven survivors from a ditched B-17, shepherding the amphibian as it flew back to Rimini.

The 304th BW was treated to a 55-aeroplane escort to Gyor, in Hungary, on 21 October, while Capt Vernon Haywood led four P-51s to search for downed fliers in the Gulf of Venezia that afternoon. They spotted two men in 'Mae Wests', and their report brought an RAF Walrus to the scene 75 minutes later, and the downed aviators were soon rescued.

MORE LOSSES

Losses resumed on 23 October during an escort mission for the Regensburg-bound 304th BW. A total of 64 Mustangs rendezvoused with the bombers despite bad weather, but during the run in to the target 2Lt Fred Brewer of the 100th FS was seen spinning into the clouds, having possibly fallen victim to flak. Brewer was killed in the subsequent crash. In addition, Robert C Chandler and Shelby Westbrook's P-51Cs were lost when the former suffered engine trouble and his escort, Westbrook, had his instruments malfunction. At low altitude and with a descending ceiling, the pair crash-landed in Yugoslavia, but evaded capture and returned to the group after 31 days on the ground.

On the 29th, Capt Alfonso Davis, who had assumed command of the 99th FS upon Lawrence's death, was himself killed during a three-ship mission escorting an F-5 Lightning in the Munich area. He had possibly fallen victim to oxygen deprivation. William Campbell, who at 25 was the oldest member of the squadron, became the new CO.

The 332nd had lost 15 pilots in October, which was a rate of attrition that Col Davis admitted was 'hard to take'. Additionally, 'the Army Air Force screwed up the pilot training production so very much that by the winter of 1944-45, there weren't any replacements, and our pilots were doing 70 missions while other fighter groups' pilots were going home after 50 missions. You can imagine the effect this had on morale'. Thanks to the still-segregated nature of training, these manpower shortages would continue until war's end.

TIGHTENING THE NOOSE

After a trio of missions on 1 November, escorting the 304th BW to Vienna and covering two supply drops to partisans in Yugoslavia, the group prepared for a change of command. On 3 November, Col Davis returned to the USA and Maj 'Spanky' Roberts once again assumed command. Weather slowed the pace of operations slightly, but on 4 November 61 Mustangs, led by Capt Andrew Turner, covered the 5th BW's attack on the Regensburg/Winterhafen oil storage facility.

Mysteriously, 20 minutes after taking off from Ramitelli, a Mustang with the same group markings as the 332nd FG, but without side numbers, joined the formation for 45 minutes before turning northeast at Trieste and disappearing. Elsewhere, Louis Purnell and Milton Brooks

On 3 November 1944, Col Davis returned to the USA and Maj 'Spanky' Roberts assumed command in his absence for the third time. Roberts would turn over command once again on Davis' return, but was given command yet again on 9 June 1945 and oversaw the return of the group to America four months later (*National Museum of the USAF*)

During the return from a mission on 7 November 1944, Fifteenth Air Force photographer Frank Ambrose radioed the fighters escorting these 465th BG Liberators and asked if they wanted to pose for some shots. The result was this image of a 100th FS Mustang zooming over the group – something that probably would not have been possible had Col Davis been leading that day (*Frank Ambrose*)

each led fighter escorts for lone reconnaissance F-5 Lightnings during the afternoon.

The next day, 48 Mustangs again 'rode herd' on the 5th BW, this time to the Florisdorf oil refinery in Austria. Lee Rayford led the uneventful mission, which was followed in the afternoon by two more F-5 escorts.

Missions in support of the 5th BW's B-17s continued on 6 November, when 63 P-51s escorted them to the Moosbierbaum oil refinery in Vienna. During the mission, P-51C 42-103974, flown by Capt William J Faulkner of the 301st, was seen falling in a tight spin near Reichenfels, in Austria. He was classified as killed in action.

Capt William Campbell commanded the 63 Mustangs that escorted the 55th BW to Trento and Bolzano, in Italy, on 7 November, and four of the P-51s suffered slight flak damage during the course of the mission. The group was then grounded by weather for 72 hours, but on the 11th, 52 Mustangs escorted 5th BW 'heavies' that struck the Brux oil refineries. Flak over Salzburg was heavy, and although 2Lt Elton H Nightengale's P-51B was last seen over friendly territory in no apparent trouble, he never returned from the mission. Turner W Payne's aeroplane also ran into trouble, and he was forced to crash-land at Lesina, destroying the Mustang but emerging from the incident unhurt.

Weather prevented any further missions being flown until 16 November, when the group escorted the 304th BW to the Munich West railway marshalling yard. During take-off, a farmer absentmindedly drove a herd of sheep across the end of the runway at Ramitelli, and the animals were hit by Roger Romine's P-51D 44-14470. The machine (one of the first D-models to be issued to the group) was in turn rammed by William Hill's P-51C-10 34-25116, causing an immense explosion. Hill, although

badly burned, was rescued by Woody Crockett, who was not scheduled to fly but was watching the take-off. Sadly, Romine died in the tangled wreckage of his flaming aircraft.

The mission pressed on, meeting up with the B-24s at Masseria. South of Latisano, a pair of Bf 109Gs (almost certainly ANR aircraft flown by Capitano Ugo Drago and Tenente Renato Mingozi) positioned themselves up-sun and at 'six o'clock' to a formation of six Mustangs and made a diving attack. They succeeded in damaging George Haley's aeroplane before P-51s from the 52nd FG chased them off.

This was not the only enemy activity the group would see on the 16th, for after the bombers had hit the target, Melvin Jackson, Louis Purnell and Luke Weathers spotted a crippled B-24 in the Udine area. Whilst attempting to protect the bomber, the three pilots were jumped by eight Bf 109s, which attacked in a string but then broke into a Lufbery for mutual defence.

A striking view of the 100th FS before a mission in November 1944, taken from the top hatch of a 465th BG Liberator. According to the photographer, the bomber crew was unaware of the presence of an all-black unit in theatre until they needed to have the B-24's wheels dug out of the mud and shouted for assistance! (*Frank Ambrose*)

At the end of an uneventful escort (evidenced by the presence of the drop tanks), the same 100th FS Mustang seen in the photograph on page 87 returns to Ramitelli (*Frank Ambrose*)

Weathers charged into the formation and closed to within 100 yards of the last two, firing short bursts with zero to 20 degrees of deflection. One of the Bf 109s began smoking and Weathers followed it from 24,000 ft down to a 1000 ft, where he saw it hit the ground. As tracers suddenly arced past his canopy, he realised that another Bf 109 had followed him down. 'It looked like they had me, so I decided to follow the falling aeroplane', Weathers said. 'I made a dive, came out of it and looked back. One aeroplane was still on my tail. I was headed back towards Germany, but I didn't want to go that way. I chopped my throttle and dropped my flaps to cut my speed quickly. The fellow overshot me, and this left me on his tail. He was in range, so I opened fire'. Several bursts resulted in the Bf 109 slamming into the side of a mountain.

The next day, Ed Gleed led 44 P-51s as escorts for the 5th BW on an attack on the Brux refineries, and while the 332nd FG reached the escort area 40 minutes late, the bombers were themselves a further ten minutes behind them because they too had been delayed by the same headwind that had slowed down the fighters.

On 18 November, Maj Roberts headed 44 Mustangs escorting a bombing strike on airfields near Verona and Vicenza. Francis Peoples launched late in P-51C 41-903942, and he was last seen hurrying to catch the group. He never rendezvoused with the 332nd and never returned to base. Lt Alva Temple's landing gear malfunctioned and he had to belly his Mustang in at Ramitelli after the mission.

STRAFERS

The next day, the group was ordered to strafe railway, road and river traffic around Gyor, in Hungary, and Vienna and Esztergom, in Austria. While the 302nd provided top cover, the 99th worked over a stretch

A 100th FS armourer reloads the trays of his B-model Mustang with ammunition at Ramitelli at the height of the airfield strafing campaign in the autumn of 1944 (*National Museum of the USAF*)

between Gyor and Veszprem, destroying 15 horse-drawn vehicles and 20 goods wagons, and damaging a further 100 horse-drawn vehicles, two locomotives, 40 goods wagons and ten trucks.

The 100th also strafed rail and road traffic, destroying one tank wagon and damaging 30 goods wagons. It then turned its attention to river traffic between Esztergom and Gyor, damaging six barges and a tugboat. During one pass, Lt Roger B Gaither's Mustang was hit by flak, and he spent the rest of the war as a PoW.

The 301st had been providing top cover for the 100th throughout their strafing attacks, and when the latter squadron had used up its ammunition, the former dropped down and resumed wreaking havoc on the river traffic. Its pilots shot up two 88 mm guns on a German lighter and damaged an additional six barges. On the way home, a burst of flak disrupted Quitman C Walker's flight from the 100th FS, damaging his aircraft enough to force him to bail out near Lake Balaton. He was never seen again.

On 20 November, Capt Rayford led 50 Mustangs covering the 5th and 55th BWs' attack on the Blechammer South oil refinery. At about the time of the rendezvous with the bombers, 1Lt Maceo Harris went missing in P-51C 42-103951 and was never seen again

Weather limited the group's activities for the rest of the month to an escort of two B-25s to Yugoslavia on 22 November and a photo-reconnaissance escort to Grodenwoh and Nurnberg four days later.

2 December saw 51 aircraft under 'Red' Jackson's control escort B-24s of the 49th and 55th BWs to Blechammer's oil refineries. Just before leaving the bombers, Lt Cornelius P Gould's coolant system gave out, belching white glycol vapour. Gould parachuted into the hands of the Germans and spent the remainder of the war in Stalag Luft I. The next day, 64 Mustangs shepherded the 49th BW through the Udine area. On this day, the only German aeroplanes spotted were six aircraft on the bombed field at Maniago.

There were losses, nevertheless. During a routine transition flight onto the Mustang, 302nd FS newcomers 2Lt Earl B Highbaugh (in P-51C 43-25118) and Flt Off James C Ramsey (in P-51C 43-25129) were killed in a mid-air collision near Ramitelli.

Weather prevented operations until 9 December, when the group mounted a 57-aeroplane escort of the 5th BW on a raid on Brux. As the B-17s and Mustangs approached the target, a single aircraft made a fast

Four P-51s swoop across the airfield at Ramitelli at the end of an escort mission in late 1944. Until weather began to close in, the group was mounting near-daily escort missions of 45 or more aircraft (*Frank Ambrose*)

Their noses pointing into the wind, a dozen Mustangs of the 100th FS, with 'Jug' Turner's *Skipper's Darlin' III* at the far left, have their engines run up before a mission in November 1944 (*Frank Ambrose*)

pass at the fighters, then 'split-S'ed' into a cloud bank, before climbing steeply back through the formation. The group had just seen its first Me 262 jet fighter. Minutes later, over Muhldorf, a second Me 262 made a head-on pass at a flight of Mustangs, and two groups of Me 262s were then spotted east of the formation. On the way home, Lt Robert Martin's Mustang suffered engine trouble, which forced him to make a wheels-down landing at the gunnery range at Cuetelo, north of Termoli. The P-51 nosed over on the rough ground and damaged the propeller.

The mission to Moosbierbaum on 11 December saw 51 Mustangs under the command of Capt Walter Downs covering the 47th BW. The rendezvous was made cleanly, and the mission's only notable incident was the sight of a B-24 exploding suddenly near Vienna. That same day Capt Claude Govan led a five-ship escort for an F-5 mission to Prague, which went without a hitch. This run of uneventful missions continued four days later when the 47th BW's strike on Innsbruck was covered by 48 Mustangs.

On 16 December, 49 Mustangs led by Maj Roberts shepherded the 5th BW's B-17s on a mission to Brux. Two of the group's aircraft were despatched to escort a crippled B-24 that stumbled along the mission's path. Other than having to divert to a secondary target at Karlovac, the mission was a milk run. That afternoon, Capt Mattison led a five-ship escort for a B-25 headed for Mrkopij, in Yugoslavia. The following day, 40 P-51s escorted the 304th BW to Olomouc, where the group spotted about 40 aeroplanes on an airfield that had been immobilised due to a lack of fuel caused by the Fifteenth Air Force's continual punishment of the German oil and lubricants infrastructure.

Another mission to Blechammer on 18 December saw 45 Mustangs arrive at the rendezvous point, which was bereft of B-24s from the 49th BW. After orbiting for 15 minutes, Capt Lee Rayford sent 32 P-51s to the target area, while the remaining 13 circled in the rendezvous area. Five minutes later, one bomb group of B-24s arrived, and they were escorted to the target. That same day, Capt William Campbell led six Mustangs on an F-5 escort to Innsbruck, where they found no flak and were not enticed lower by the sight of three locomotives running in broad daylight.

Blechammer South oil refinery was targeted 24 hours later by B-24s from the 55th BW, the bombers arriving 17 minutes late. This in turn forced the group's 57 Mustangs to give up the escort just after the wing reached the target area. Elsewhere, 1Lt Alva Temple led five Mustangs that morning to cover an F-5 mission to Dresden which proved uneventful. The next day, another mission had to be cut short when the

5th BW was 15 minutes late arriving at the rendezvous. The briefed target was Brux, but one group broke north for the secondary target of Salzburg, while the rest of the 'heavies' headed for Regensburg. Two Mustangs were forced down at forward airfields through a shortage of fuel.

The group's reconnaissance escort missions were by now becoming commonplace, and on 20 December Lt Charles Dunne's flight covered an F-5 sent to overfly Prague. Two days later Lt George Gray and his five Mustangs protected another F-5 photographing Ingolstadt. On the 23rd it was Capt Andrew Turner's turn to lead a five-ship mission escorting yet another Prague-bound F-5. On the latter flight, Capt Lawrence Dickson's P-51D 44-15144, developed engine trouble near the target area and he bailed out over the Alps. Although Dickson's parachute was seen to open, he was later found frozen to death.

On Christmas Eve, the group received a present when Col Benjamin Davis returned from the USA and resumed command of the 332nd. The next morning, 42 Mustangs, again led by Turner, covered the 'heavies' visiting Brux. On the way home, the group spotted four Bf 109s below them chasing seven B-26s, and a section of fighters peeled off to intercept. As the Mustangs dived on them, the Messerschmitts broke off their attack and fled the area.

Groundcrew-eyes' view of the 100th FS , with 'Jug' Turner in the lead. Turner remained in the USAAF after the war, only to perish in the crash of a P-47N in 1947 (*Frank Ambrose*)

A 99th FS P-51D sits at Ramitelli between missions in November 1944. As the pace of operations intensified, the blue-and-white chequered sash around the nose of squadron aircraft gave way to a simpler band of light blue (*National Museum of the USAF*)

Another photograph of 'Jug' Turner's P-51C *Skipper's Darlin' III*, taken just prior to a mission in the autumn of 1944. Turner's crew chief appears to be applying a tape covering to the fighter's gun ports. This quick job was always done just prior to the fighter taxiing out, the tape helping to reduce the chances of moisture collecting in the barrels of the 0.50-cal weapons and then turning to solid ice at altitude, rendering the guns inoperable (*Jon Lake Collection*)

26 December saw the group provide a two-pronged escort for the 5th and 55th BWs, sent to attack targets in Odertal and Blechammer. The 100th and 301st sent 23 Mustangs in one group and the 99th and 302nd provided 21 Mustangs for withdrawal cover. Both groups found the bombers' formations to be good and tight, making them easy to cover. This contrasted markedly with the 5th BW's B-17s the next day, which the escorting force of 52 P-51s, led by Capt Ed Gleed, found strung out over several miles on the way to their targets in Vienna. Luckily, no enemy aircraft rose to take advantage of the situation.

On the 28th, the 304th BW hit the oil refineries at Kolin and Pardubice, in Czechoslovakia. Fifty 332nd FG Mustangs covered the mission, and when the bombers split into two groups, they split with them – another example of their excellent escort tactics.

A replay of that mission was scheduled for 29 December, with the targets this time being Muhldorf and Landshut, in Germany. The 304th BW rendezvoused with the 332nd, and almost immediately 11 Mustangs were detached to escort a single 49th BW B-24 in an attack on Passau. Over the target, Lts Frederick D Funderberg and Andrew Marshall of the 301st were last seen at around 1155 hrs. Minutes later they fell victim to either flak or a mid-air collision, and both were killed. On the return flight to Ramitelli, Lt Robert Friend's aircraft entered a spin and he bailed out over Larino, and Lt Lewis Craig bailed out over Termoli. Both men duly returned to their squadron.

The weather moved in on 30 December, giving the pilots of the 332nd FG a brief respite from this gruelling series of four-hour bomber escort missions.

In his year-end message to the group, Col Davis stressed that the 332nd's record for escort was not going unnoticed. 'Unofficially, you are known by an untold number of bomber crews as those who can be depended on, and whose appearance means certain protection from enemy fighters', Davis wrote. 'The bomber crews have told others of your accomplishments, and your good reputation has preceded you in many parts where you may think you are unknown'.

GRINDING DOWN THE REICH

Weather limited the group to just 11 missions in January 1945, but it brought no respite to the comings and goings of personnel at Ramitelli. The first to go was Maj Lee Rayford, CO of the 301st, who returned home and was replaced by Capt Armour McDaniel. Just days later, Capt Melvin Jackson turned command of the 302nd over to Capt Vernon Haywood. The group also managed to temporarily ease its pilot shortage when 34 new aviators arrived from the USA.

The 332nd remained grounded until 3 January, when Lt Alfred Gorham led a three-Mustang flight that accompanied an F-5 to Munich and Linz. However, cloud cover over Austria and southern Germany forced the mission to be abandoned. A second attempt to make the same run, this time with a photo-reconnaissance Mosquito, also ran into bad weather and yielded no results.

Sgts Calvin P Thierry, William E Pitts, Harold Cobb and an unidentified fourth man perform maintenance on one of the group's Mustangs. Although the initial months with the P-51 were fraught with serviceability problems, the group soon had a maintenance record the equal of any in the MTO (*National Museum of the USAF*)

Weather continued to foil the group's efforts on 8 January, when the 47th BW attempted to strike the Linz railway marshalling yard. The 51 Mustangs that reached the rendezvous point found no bombers, for the B-24s had made a 360-degree turn when they encountered solid overcast upon making landfall. The bombers and fighters never spotted each other, and the Mustangs were all back on the ground by 1450 hrs.

One week later, the group tried again. Col Davis led 52 Mustangs to the rendezvous point, only to find no trace of the 304th BW's B-24s. The colonel had the group orbit once, before rendezvousing with a wing of B-24s – oddly enough from the 47th BW! The Liberators were escorted as far as the Mustangs' fuel would allow, before being turned free.

Freddie Hutchins led the photo-reconnaissance escort mission on 18 January, and once again the F-5 and its escorts reached the target – Stuttgart – only to find it completely covered in cloud. At about the same time, six more Mustangs commanded by Capt William Campbell chaperoned an F-5 to Munich, where the weather allowed the Lightning to make its photo run. Elsewhere that same day, Lt Howard Gamble and his wingman escorted an F-5 to Prague. Cloud cover up to 34,000 ft forced the reconnaissance pilot to give up the mission, and ten minutes later the F-5's right engine started to splutter. The escorts could only watch helplessly as the Lightning descended inexorably toward the undercast. At 29,000 ft the pilot radioed, 'This is it – I'm going to bail out. Tell them back at the field that I will be alright'.

On 20 January the 99th FS came close to suffering its own non-combat losses during a reconnaissance mission. Capt George Gray had led four P-51s and an F-5 Lightning to Prague, but during the withdrawal from the target area, the five aircraft ran into a snowstorm while flying at just 300 ft above the ground. The pilots became separated, and somehow they all managed to navigate their way home in terrible weather – the last aeroplane landed after seven-and-a-half hours in the air.

Twenty minutes after Gray's photo-reconnaissance flight took off, Capt Gleed led 46 Mustangs on an escort mission for the 5th BW, which was attacking oil storage facilities near Regensburg. Although no enemy aircraft rose to challenge the group, flak was heavy, damaging a P-51 and perhaps also accounting for Flt Off Samuel J Foreman and 2Lt Albert L Young. Both were recorded as missing, and were later confirmed as having been killed.

On 21 January, 44 Mustangs provided high cover for the 5th BW's attack on refineries in Austria. When the bombers radioed ahead that they were 30 minutes late, the group proceeded to the target area and the 'heavies' caught up with them there. On the way to the target two Me 262s were spotted, but they remained out of range.

Following this mission, the weather closed in. Ten days would pass before the Fifteenth Air Force could again mount a major attack on Axis targets. Finally, on the 31st, the 47th and 55th BWs struck the Moosbierbaum oil refinery, in Austria. The wings arrived 15 and 30 minutes late to the rendezvous point, but Capt Vernon Haywood and his 42 Mustangs reacted flexibly, splitting into two groups to cover both formations' approaches to the target.

On 1 February, the Fifteenth Air Force launched a 'one-two' punch on Moosbierbaum. Col Davis led an escort of 100th and 301st fighters for the

49th BW, whose bomber crews seemed confused when it came to determining their target. With the minutes ticking by as the 'heavies' circled over Austria looking for their initial point, Davis had to pass responsibility for withdrawal escort cover over to another Mustang group. An hour after this first mission started, the 99th and 302nd FSs launched their fighters from Ramitelli under the command of Capt Gwynne Peirson. Their job would be to escort the 47th BW,

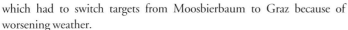

2Lt Bob Lawrence of the 301st clowns for the camera in front of his P-51C-10-NT 44-11086 *Rick Lizzie* in February 1945 (*via Jack Morris*)

which had to switch targets from Moosbierbaum to Graz because of worsening weather.

Four Mustangs, led by Lt Harold Morris, flew an uneventful F-5 escort to Salzburg two days later, and on the 5th, the group escorted the 47th BW as its bombers attacked the Salzburg Main Railway Station using reconnaissance photographs from this mission. Terrible weather en route to the target area scattered the fighters and prevented an effective escort from being flown. Luckily, no enemy fighters challenged the unprotected bomber formations.

Three days later, weather again disrupted a planned fighter sweep to clear opposition for a supply drop to partisans in Yugoslavia, the 12 Mustangs sortied finding clouds that stretched from the mountain tops up to 30,000 ft. Communication problems also meant that the pilots could not contact the transport aircraft by radio.

On 7 February, the Fifteenth Air Force again tried a two-pronged attack on Moosbierbaum. The early flight, under Capt George Gray, saw 33 99th and 302nd FS Mustangs escorting the 304th BW, and an hour later Capt Andrew 'Jug' Turner led 29 fighters from the 100th and 301st FSs accompanying the 47th BW's B-24s. The latter formation came under anti-aircraft fire around Vienna, and two Mustangs shepherded a flak-damaged bomber to the safety of the forward field at Ancona.

BETTER WEATHER, MORE MISSIONS

As the weather cleared, the pace of operations quickened. Following another F-5 escort on 8 February, Lt Spurgeon Ellington led a replay of the weather-plagued supply drop mission to Yugoslavia. This time, the 12 fighters found the weather favourable, and after the Mustangs had verified the absence of German forces, they watched as an RAF Lysander came into the area and landed in a field. That same day, 41 Mustangs under Maj Roberts' control escorted the 55th BW's attack on the Vienna South goods and ordnance depots.

Although combat fatalities were now in decline, the 99th lost a new pilot on 11 February when 2Lt Thomas C Street was killed when his Mustang crashed during a transitional flight. The next day, Capt Alva Temple led a six-aircraft escort of an F-5, which made three runs over Linz – the final one coming after it was discovered that its primary target, Prague, was socked in. Capt Freddie Hutchins led the next day's reconnaissance escort, shepherding an F-5 to Munich. That same morning, 45 Mustangs accompanied the 49th BW to the Vienna central railway repair works, followed two hours later by a separate 12-ship escort for bombers attacking targets in Zagreb, Maribor and Graz.

14 February saw plenty of activity for the wing once again, with Col Davis leading 30 Mustangs as escorts for the 5th BW raid on the Vienna Lobau and Schwechat oil refineries. During the course of the mission, two Mustangs were detached to cover a group of B-17s that had become separated from the main force while dodging flak, and the rest of the 100th and 301st FS fighters became separated from the bombers in the target area by cloud cover. Fortunately, they were able to rejoin after the bomb run. A B-17 and a B-24 that were straggling behind the main formation were also chaperoned to safety.

Once the bombers were safely out of Austria, three other Mustangs dropped down and strafed five small craft on the Drava River, although no damage appeared to have been inflicted on the vessels. 'Spanky' Roberts led the uneventful second half of the mission, with 36 Mustangs from the 99th and 302nd escorting the 55th BW to the same targets.

Another staggered mission was flown on 15 February, this time to the Penzinger railway marshalling yard in Vienna. Capt Vernon Haywood led 32 Mustangs of the 99th and 302nd aloft at 1030 hrs to escort the 49th BW's Red Force, and a hour later Andrew Turner's formation of 100th and 301st P-51s lifted off to accompany the 49th BW's Blue Force. Turner's formation saw the only 'hostile' aircraft to present themselves – a pair of confused P-38s which made two ineffective passes at the Mustangs. Again, the 332nd provided cover to cripples from the 451st and 461st BGs.

Spann Watson led the escorts for a photo escort mission on 16 February, during which a Mosquito made several passes over Memmingen airfield, and Lt Alfonso Simmons led the second six-aeroplane escort which took an F-5 to the Munich area. Just after Watson's formation departed, the group launched 49 Mustangs for a 5th BW escort mission to Lechfeld airfield, but weather scattered the 332nd

Armourers re-arm one of the group's P-51B/Cs (a hand-me-down from the 52nd FG, judging by its wing bands). The angled installation of the P-51B/C's guns led to jams – something the 332nd's armourers had to contend with until VE-Day (*National Museum of the USAF*)

99th FS crew chief Sgt William Accoo washes his Mustang between missions. The pride taken by the enlisted men of the group is evident in the shine on the aeroplane's fuselage skinning – it is bright enough to see Accoo in the reflection (*National Air and Space Museum*)

so badly that only nine P-51s, led by Lt Emile Clifton, rendezvoused with the bombers. 2Lt John H Chavis of the 99th FS went missing in P-51C 42-103914 shortly after the group departed from Ramitelli, and he was never seen again.

Two reconnaissance escort missions were performed on the morning of the 17th – a six-aeroplane escort of an F-5 to Nurnberg and a four-fighter escort of a Mosquito to Munich. An hour after these missions were launched, 44 P-51s took off from Ramitelli and headed for the Linz-Vienna railway line, looking for targets to strafe. Once in the area, the squadron formations took turns in strafing and providing top cover for each other as they attacked four trains. The 99th and 302nd made three passes on targets while the 100th and 301st each made two. The group claimed two locomotives, two trucks on flat cars, three tank wagons and a power transformer destroyed, plus three locomotives, seven tanks on flat cars, 15 trucks on flat cars, five tank wagons, 15 goods wagons, five armoured cars on flat cars, a railway control tower and a small factory damaged. No Mustangs were lost during the mission.

The next day, Lt Elwood Driver led the by now routine reconnaissance mission, his three Mustangs taking an F-5 to Linz. Col Davis, meanwhile, led 53 P-51s later that day on an escort mission for the 47th BW as it attacked the Wels railway marshalling yard. However, after a hazardous climb out through thick overcast, the pilots heard the weather aircraft transmit the recall signal to the bombers, scrubbing the mission.

On 19 February, the group sent 48 Mustangs aloft, and this time weather permitted a rendezvous, although it was a sloppy one thanks to headwinds that delayed both the fighters and bombers. At one point, a single Spitfire started to make a pass on the formation, but when three Mustangs dropped tanks and broke into him, the British fighter 'split-S'ed' away.

Driver again commanded the photo-reconnaissance escort on the 20th, which saw five Mustangs shepherding an F-5 to Nurnberg, One of the F-5's engines began running rough before reaching the target, however, and the formation turned back – the Lightning landed safely at San Severo. That afternoon, Capt Turner commanded 43 Mustangs escorting the 47th BW to Vipitento and Brenner railway marshalling yards. The 332nd was on time for the rendezvous, but no bombers could be found. Turner ordered one-third of his fighters onto the target area, while the rest

orbited over the rendezvous point – they were joined by the Liberators six minutes later.

The weather again proved difficult, and the bombers finally headed for their number five target (Fiume), at which point the escorts had to leave for home. The first group of 11 fighters provided penetration escort to a group from the 49th BW, which was attacking the original target.

Armour McDaniel led the 21 February mission, which sent 39 Mustangs north with the 304th BW to the Vienna central railway marshalling yard. One of the B-24s had mechanical difficulties and left the formation just as the fighters rendezvoused with the bombers – two Mustangs were despatched to see the Liberator safely to Trieste. The rest of the mission progressed without incident.

On the 22nd, the group was tasked with escorting the 5th BW's attack on railway marshalling yards in southwest Germany, followed by a strafing mission against rail targets. The 44 Mustangs shepherded the bombers to the target, but the strafing mission was called off when the target area was found to be completely socked in. Reconnaissance escorts later in the day targeted Prague and Stuttgart, with 1Lt Clifton and Capt Driver leading the Mustangs. The next day's mission to cover the 304th BW's attack on the Gmund West railway marshalling yard was again hampered by weather – the B-24s were forced to split up and hit two alternate targets, but Col Davis kept the escorts in place for both groups of B-24s.

1Lt Spurgeon Ellington commanded a five-aeroplane escort for a Mosquito reconnaissance mission to Munich on 24 February, and a six-aeroplane escort for an F-5 visit to the city the next afternoon. Some of the information gathered on these flights may have led to the mission of 25 February, when 45 P-51s were despatched to strafe

Tyre blowouts were always a threat on Ramitelli's PSP runway. This Mustang's badly-blown starboard tyre is being replaced by a trio of men the old-fashioned way – with plenty of muscle (*National Museum of the USAF*)

A 99th FS Mustang lands back at Ramitelli following an escort mission in early 1945. The presence of its tanks hints at the growing impotence of the Luftwaffe (*National Air and Space Museum*)

traffic in the Munich-Linz-Ingol-stadt Salzburg area.

The 99th, 100th and 301st FSs assumed their usual strafing tactics, with squadrons alternating between strafing and providing top cover. The 100th started the destruction, dropping down to strike the line running between Rosenheim, Muhldorf and Landshut. The attack destroyed four locomotives and damaged three others, and five passenger carriages, six oil wagons, four goods wagons and a pair of ore wagons were also damaged. Unit records also note that three soldiers were hit.

A 100th FS Mustang 'rides herd' on a 450th BG Liberator somewhere over the Alps in early 1945. Red-tailed Mustangs were among the favourite sights enjoyed by Fifteenth Air Force bomber crews (*Stanley Purwinis via Tom Purwinis*)

In the midst of the attack, an aerodrome was spotted with 15 aircraft scattered about – in short order, two He 111s were in flames and a third He 111 and a Bf 109 were damaged.

As the 100th rose to assume top cover duties, the 99th descended on the railway line, destroying six locomotives and shooting up 40 goods wagons, five passenger carriages, four trucks and an additional locomotive. In the process, however, 2Lt George Iles' P-51 was hit in the coolant system by flak and he bailed out. Although the pilot attempted to escape to Switzerland, he was captured in southern Germany.

2Lt Wendell Hockaday was so intent on hitting a locomotive that he actually flew into it, ripping off part of his wing. He nursed the Mustang as far as the Alps before bailing out near Vitendorf, but he was never seen alive again. Flak also damaged 2Lt Daniel L Rich's P-51 – he crash-landed in a valley north of Campomarino, in Italy, and escaped with second-degree burns to his face.

The 301st came down next, but fuel limited them to five minutes of strafing. An electrical power station was damaged, another destroyed and an electric locomotive was peppered with 0.50-cal machine gun rounds. While the 99th was making its passes, 1Lt Alfred Gorham's P-51 suffered an engine failure and he was forced to bail out just east of Munich. He was soon captured and spent the rest of the war as a PoW.

In the wake of this costly mission, the group was thankful to return to a round of photo-reconnaissance escort flights and bomber escort duties. 1Lt Richard Harder led the three-aeroplane escort for a PR Mosquito to Munich on 26 February, whilst the following day, 32 Mustangs under Maj Roberts' command accompanied the 49th BW to Augsberg railway marshalling yard. The last day of February featured an F-5 escort to Prague, led by 1Lt Chris Newman, a second reconnaissance escort to Prague later that same day, led by 1Lt Albert Manning, and a 34-aeroplane escort of the 5th BW to Verona, led by Col Davis.

The personnel problems that continued to plague the group had led to a virtual deactivation of the 302nd in February, and on 6 March the unit was officially taken off the mission roster and its pilots assigned to the three remaining squadrons.

In the final weeks of the war, as German forces were squeezed into an ever-shrinking area, the group would see increasing opposition.

JETS AND JUBILATION

Although it was becoming clear that conflict in Europe was nearing its end, German resolve showed no sign of cracking. Similarly, the pressures on the group from operational accidents continued unabated. During March, Flt Off Thomas L Hawkins was killed when his Mustang crashed on take-off and, even more disheartening, 1Lt Roland W Moody died of burns that he received when a drop tank fell off an aircraft as it taxied by and burst when it struck the pilot's tent.

The month started with the now-routine reconnaissance escorts to Prague and Stuttgart, complementing a 39-aeroplane escort to Moosbierbaum for the 55th BW. When the Vienna area was found to be completely socked in, the wing bombed the alternate target at Amstetten. The situation facing the Germans was highlighted by the sight of a dozen Il-2 *Sturmoviks* spotted in the air just prior to the P-51s rendezvousing with the bombers.

On 2 March the group sent out Mustangs to protect an F-5 mission to Prague, followed by an uneventful 34-aeroplane escort for the 304th BW to the Linz railway marshalling yard, led by Capt Jack Holsclaw. The next morning, the 100th and 301st sent 23 aeroplanes to scour the area between Bruck and Weiner-Neustadt, in Austria, for trains to strafe. Flying along the Maribor-Graz line, the 100th sent four aeroplanes down to shoot up parked rolling stock, and seven goods wagons and a passenger carriage were damaged.

Seven more Mustangs overflew the area between Gliesdorf and Radkersberg but found nothing. A second section continued north past Bruek, then turned south and finally found parked goods wagons on a siding near Langenwang, damaging two of them. Eight more of the 100th's Mustangs remained in the Graz area, and two of them, flown by Lts Robert Martin and Alphonso Simmons, dropped down to attack an airfield south of Graz. Both men, who were last seen starting their strafing runs, quickly fell to flak. Simmons was killed, but Martin, who radioed 'I will walk in from here' just after his aeroplane was hit, made good on that statement, returning to the group in April.

Col Benjamin O Davis leads a briefing in the spring of 1945. The respect Davis commanded had a direct impact on the group's adherence to his 'escort at all cost' approach (*National Museum of the USAF*)

Col Davis led the mission of 4 March which saw 42 Mustangs escort the 49th BW to the Graz railway marshalling yards yet again. The next day, five P-51s escorted a Mosquito to photograph the area around Munich – a mission duplicated on 7 March, but this time with an F-5. Forty-eight hours later, the photographic subjects were Linz and Munich – all these missions passed without incident.

The third mission on 9 March took 39 Mustangs to the Bruck marshalling yards with the 5th BW, the escorts splitting into two forces to give the bombers coverage over the target for the full duration of their attack.

On 12 March, another pair of F-5 escorts was carried out, again to Linz and Munich, followed by a 48-aeroplane mission led by Capt William Campbell to the Florisdorf oil refinery, near Vienna. While escorting the 47th BW on the latter operation, two bogies were spotted on the deck. A pair of Mustangs were sent down to investigate, but they lost the aircraft in ground haze. Later, the group heard over the radio that a B-24 was being attacked by enemy fighters, but it was unable to ascertain where the bomber was located.

From 13 March, the routine F-5 escorts started to become more interesting. The early flight to Stuttgart that day went as planned, but one member of a six-aeroplane escort for the photo-reconnaissance mission to Nurnberg found more action than he expected. The unnamed Mustang pilot took off late and was hurrying to catch up with the rest of his formation when a single Fw 190 dived on him. When the pilot dropped his tanks and turned into the enemy, he spotted a second Focke-Wulf diving out of the sun from about his 'four o'clock'. The pilot 'split S-ed' for the deck, with the Fw 190s in pursuit, but upon reaching the coast the German pilots abandoned the chase.

Ed Gleed led the day's escort mission, taking three groups of bombers from the 5th BW to the Regensburg railway marshalling yard. The formation spotted two Fw 190s, but they were too distant to be engaged by the fighters.

14 March proved to be an exceptionally busy day for the group, with four missions scheduled. Two were photo-reconnaissance escorts for Mosquitoes heading to Munich about one hour apart. The day's major assignment tasked the 100th and 301st with shepherding the 47th BW to the Varazdin railway bridge and marshalling yard. That mission went without incident, but the 21 aircraft of the 99th assigned to strafe targets on the Bruck-Leoben-Steyr railway line that morning saw enough action for the entire group.

Despite moderate, accurate, light flak at Hieflau, the squadron destroyed nine locomotives and nine goods wagons, and damaged a further nine locomotives, 127 goods wagons, 37 flat cars, eight oil wagons, seven trucks on flat cars, three railway stations, two railway buildings, a power station and a warehouse, which was left burning.

During one pass, P-51D 44-25070, flown by 99th FS pilot Harold Brown, was hit and and the latter was forced to bail out. Pilots saw him running for cover in the snow halfway up the side of a mountain, but only 30 minutes after he had landed, two constables apprehended him and marched him back to Hieflau, where an angry mob awaited. The mob had a rope, and they dragged Brown to a small tree and prepared to hang him.

Luckily, a third constable arrived with a rifle and forced the mob to back down. The constable delivered Brown to the military police in a nearby town, who interned him in Stalag Luft I for the remaining weeks of the war in Europe.

The next day, Capt Downs led eight Mustangs on a 'special mission' to Yugoslavia. While on station, Downs spotted eight B-24s and five Halifaxes, plus another escorting group of four Spitfires, all of which were participating in yet more re-supply sorties for partisans. Just before this mission was launched, 49 additional Mustangs under Capt Woodrow Crockett had set out to rendezvous with the 5th BW, which was attacking Zittau, in Germany.

On 16 March, 31 aircraft were sent to strafe rail targets in Austria and Germany. Eight aeroplanes from the 99th attacked a stretch of track between Ebersberg and Neumarkt for more than an hour, while three others provided top cover. The fighters destroyed two locomotives, four

Five weary men exit the parachute shack after an early-morning briefing. The ever-present and infamous Italian mud made life difficult even at Ramitelli (*Toni Frissell via National Archives*)

trucks on flat cars and five goods wagons, and damaged a further 45 goods wagons, five locomotives and four trucks on flat cars, as well as eight buildings.

The 100th attacked a stretch of railway line to the west, sending three aeroplanes down to strafe while six others kept a lookout for the Luftwaffe. The three Mustangs destroyed two locomotives and damaged two more, as well as five goods wagons and a baggage car. The 301st strafed Plattling, with 11 Mustangs destroying three locomotives and a flak car and damaging 15 goods wagons, nine locomotives, six coal wagons, three passenger carriages, an oil wagon and the railway station.

The 301st found more targets when it reached Mettenheim airfield, where five Mustangs strafed the assembled aircraft. One fighter lined up a Bf 109 that was trying to take-off, sprayed it with machine gun fire and saw it collapse back onto the airfield. The official score was three Fw 190s and a Ju 52/3m destroyed, and nine Fw 190s, two Bf 109s, one Fw 200, an unidentified biplane trainer, two barracks buildings and an operations building damaged.

The group also repeatedly strafed a large reinforced concrete structure, which the Germans called Project *Weingut* (Wine Estate) *I* – a massive building planned as a plant for the manufacture of Me 262 engines and parts. The facility was being built by concentration camp inmates and Russian PoWs from Dachau. Only half-finished, the site was overrun by the Allies on 2 May.

The attack was not without losses, however, for 2Lt Robert C Robinson of the 100th FS, in P-51B 44-24820, was lost when, during a low strafing pass north of Muhldorf, his Mustang struck its left wing on a tree and exploded.

The next day, after more Mosquito escort missions to Munich and Prague, Lt Manning led a six-ship mission to cover the withdrawal of 70 B-24s attacking Monfalcone Harbour, in northern Italy. F-5s received escorts on 17 March too, with Prague and Linz being documented, and Mosquitoes were taken to the same targets 48 hours later.

That same day, Col Davis led a 44-aircraft escort of the 55th BW to the Muhldorf railway marshalling yard – the only enemy aeroplane sighted was a single Me 262 fighter headed away from the formation over the Brenner Pass.

A photo-escort mission to Linz and Munich in the early afternoon of 20 March and covering a supply run by a C-47 to Sanski Most, in Yugoslavia, were overshadowed by a two-part escort launched that morning. The first wave, under Capt Bill Campbell, was broken up by rough weather, but ten Mustangs rendezvoused with the 304th BW on its way to the Kralupy oil refinery – six of the fighters were subsequently forced home because of a lack of fuel. When the bombers ran into even worse weather and turned south, the four remaining Mustangs stayed with them as long as they could before turning for home and dropping to deck level. They found a seven-wagon train at Buchkirchen and destroyed the locomotive, before shooting up a pair of goods wagons.

A dozen other Mustangs missed the rendezvous entirely, and as they searched for the bombers, the engine of Lt Newman Golden's P-51B 43-7068 seized, forcing him to bail out. He floated down into German captivity. As fuel ran low, this group of Mustangs began to lose sections and flights as they broke for home, but four fighters stumbled across a 34-aeroplane formation of 49th B-24s and provided an opportunistic escort for them.

The second wave, led by Capt Ed Gleed, saw none of the problems of the first wave. The group joined up with the 304th over Lambach as assigned, and they provided an escort all the way to the alternate target – the Wels railway marshalling yard.

The seven-and-a-half-hour missions of the previous day did not keep the group down on 21 March, when 38 P-51s, commanded by Col Davis, escorted the 47th BW to another airfield in southern Germany. On the way home, two Mustangs found a lone B-24 of the 376th BG struggling along with its number two engine feathered, so they nursed it back to the airfield at Zara. Group pilots also flew three photo-escort missions that day, and another on 22 March to Ruhland, in Germany.

Twenty minutes after this mission had departed Ramitelli, 50 Mustangs launched in two forces to cover another attack by the 304th BW on the Kralupy oil refinery. The only action seen came when a trio of 52nd FG Mustangs turned into an element of the 332nd, causing a brief moment of anxiety.

The photographs taken on 22 March helped prompt the 5th BW's attack on the Ruhland oil refinery the following day, which was accompanied by 43 P-51s from the 332nd. Although no enemy aircraft were spotted, one P-51 suffered mechanical problems and its pilot, 2Lt Lincoln Hudson, turned east toward Russian lines because he lacked the altitude to cross the Alps. Eventually, Hudson bailed out of P-51C 42-103565 in the vicinity of Tropau, in Czechoslovakia, and was beaten badly by civilians before German soldiers could take him into custody. He was imprisoned in Stalag Luft III and later Stalag Luft VIIA.

LONGEST MISSION

On 24 March, the Fifteenth Air Force launched its longest mission – a 1600-mile round trip to the Daimler-Benz tank assembly plant in Berlin – which was being flown in an effort to help draw pressure off Operation *Varsity*. The latter was the codename for the Allied airborne assault on the eastern side of the Rhine. Supporting this mission were 59 Mustangs from the 332nd FG, which were tasked with escorting B-17s from the 5th BW. The group departed Ramitelli at 1145 hrs, and five aircraft aborted soon after take-off. The remaining 54 continued north, and 38 of them rendezvoused with the bombers over Kaaden, in southern Germany. Here, they relieved the P-38s of the 1st FG.

A short while later Col Davis' Mustang developed a vibration at high manifold pressure, and he relinquished the lead of the mission to Capt Armour McDaniel, CO of the 301st.

The group was scheduled to turn its escort duties over to the 31st FG on the outskirts of Berlin, but the latter group was late and the 332nd continued towards the German capital. As the combined formation neared the target area at 1208 hrs, some 25 enemy fighters (mostly Me 262s from JG 7) engaged the American bombers.

The 332nd immediately came to the aid of the 'heavies', intercepting the first pass made by a string of four Me 262s on the lower right echelon of the lead group of bombers from 'five o'clock high'. The leader of the

A small group of men listen intently to a pre-mission briefing in the 332nd's Operations Room, most likely before a photo-reconnaissance mission. Such escorts became increasingly common as 1945 wore on (*Toni Frissell via National Archives*)

four-ship formation continued down, while the next two rolled to the right and dived away from the bomber stream. The fourth Me 262 broke high and to the left.

1Lt Richard Harder tried to follow the second two jets, firing several bursts from 1000 yards down to 300 yards – he claimed to have damaged one of the aircraft. Meanwhile, Capt Edwin M Thomas had spotted the same attack. 'My entire section of eight aircraft broke after the jets', he said. He and 2Lt Vincent I Mitchell pursued the two Me 262s trying to dive away, and they also believed that they had managed to hit one of the German fighters as it fled, although there is no mention of any damage being inflicted on JG 7's Me 262s on this date in the unit's official wartime records.

Two minutes later, 1Lt Reid E Thompson of the 100th FS spotted another jet making a pass at the bombers from 'two o'clock high', so he peeled away to attack it. Another flight cut between him and his original target, so he broke off his pursuit.

Thompson then saw another aircraft which he almost certainly misidentified as an Me 163 (the only Komet launch sites within range of this combat had been overrun by this time). After Thompson fired a short burst from long range, the enemy aeroplane went into a steep dive in an effort to escape his pursuer. 'He was almost vertical in his dive', Thompson reported, and 'no smoke appeared from his jets'. The Mustang pilot pulled out of his pursuit at 6000 ft, and although he said he did not see the jet crash, he claimed that he saw smoke on the ground 'where I estimated he had hit'.

At the same time, an Me 262 made another pass at the bombers in a 30-degree dive, after which he flew right across the nose of 1Lt Earl R 'Squirrel' Lane. 'He appeared as if he was peeling off from an attack on the bombers', the pilot recalled. 'I came in for a 30-degree deflection shot from 2000 ft away. He didn't quite fill my sight. I fired three short bursts and saw the aeroplane emitting smoke. A piece of it, either the canopy or one of the jet orifices, then flew off'.

Lane achieved complete surprise over his foe, 7-kill ace Oberleutnant Alfred Ambs in Me 262A-1/R1 Wk-Nr. 110999, who had already completed two successful passes against the B-17s. 'As I flew away from the bomber stream, phosphorus shells suddenly struck my cockpit', Ambs later wrote. 'My oxygen mask was riddled and splinters struck my face. I quickly jettisoned the canopy and pulled up the nose of my Me 262 to lose speed. I bailed out at approximately 350 kph at an altitude of about 6000 metres'.

Lane broke off his attack at 17,000 ft, then pulled up and circled over the spot where Ambs' Me 262 had begun its final dive. He was rewarded with the sight of 'a crash and a puff of black smoke', followed by a second smaller impact two seconds later. Ambs came down in a tree near Wittenburg, tearing ligaments and breaking his kneecap. It would be his last flight of the war.

Meanwhile, two more Me 262s zoomed through the formation, only to find 1Lt Robert Williams and wingman Samuel Watts Jnr waiting for them. As they turned into the Me 262s, the two jets fired on Watts, whose manoeuvrability was hampered by a hung-up drop tank. When the Me 262s passed below the Mustangs, Williams 'split-S'ed' after them and got on their tails at a range of about 1500 ft. As the Me 262s opened the distance, he fired at the trailing jet and claimed damage to its tail.

1Lt Richard Harder, climbing back up to 26,000 ft after his earlier fruitless chase, spotted three more Me 262s attacking the bombers from 'five o'clock high'. The jets 'did not reach the bombers, as I turned my flight into them', he later explained. The jets made a quick right turn as Harder's 'Blue Flight' turned inside of them. They then split up, with one diving away and a second entering a steep climb. The third continued its turn, and Harder fired at him from 2000 ft down to 900 ft, observing hits on the fuselage for a second damaged claim.

Flt Off Joseph Chineworth claimed a probable at about the same time after three Me 262s turned into his flight. 'We broke right and down on them, pursuing them through a series of turns while descending', Chineworth explained. 'When I got to within 1500 ft, I started firing on the rearmost enemy aircraft. I fired three bursts and my guns stopped'. Chineworth saw pieces come off the jet and it started trailing smoke, before entering a dive at 15,000 ft.

A few minutes later, Me 262A-1a/R1 Wk-Nr. 111676 'Yellow 6', with Oberleutnant Ernst Worner at the controls, lined up for another pass on the bombers. He cut in front of Flt Off Charles Brantley's Mustang, and the young pilot firewalled his Merlin engine to close the distance. 'He was well within range when I fired four bursts', Brantley said. He then broke off his attack, but another 100th FS pilot saw Worner's jet erupt in flames and lurch out of control. The wounded German pilot was able to bail out, but his injuries prevented him from flying again.

1Lt Roscoe Brown spotted four jets heading north below the bombers and he peeled off to attack them, but 'almost immediately I saw a lone Me 262 at 24,000 ft climbing 90 degrees to me some distance from me', Brown said. 'I pulled up at him in a 15-degree climb and fired three long bursts from 2000 ft at "eight o'clock" to him'. Almost immediately, the jet's pilot, Oberleutnant Franz Kulp, bailed out of 'Yellow 5' as flames burst from the engines of the stricken jet. The wounded Kulp floated down to safety, but like his fellow pilots, the severity of his injuries meant his war had come to an end.

Despite these successes, the group did not escape unscathed from the battle, however. At 1215 hrs, flak blew off the outer right wing of Leon 'Woodie' Spears' Mustang *Kitten*. 'Looking at that wing and hearing how the engine was running, I knew there was no way I could get over the Alps to Italy', Spears recalled. Instead, he turned east and headed

Roscoe Brown poses with *BUNNIE*, which was his mount during the 24 March 1945 mission to Berlin. Brown had spotted Me 262s on previous sorties, but they had failed to engage the bombers until this mission. After 68 combat missions, Brown left the USAAF upon war's end and later served as the president of Bronx Community College of the City University of New York (*National Museum of the USAF*)

Leon 'Woodie' Spears arrived in Italy in late 1944 and flew a Mustang named *Donna* until it was written off in a landing accident. His next personal aircraft was *Kitten*, which he inherited when Charles McGee rotated home (*'Woodie' Spears*)

for the Soviet lines in Poland. Losing altitude, he selected a field near a river for a landing, only to discover that he was flying directly into a skirmish between Soviet and German troops, who held opposite banks of a nearby river. 'Between the two of them, they shot my aeroplane to pieces', Spears said. 'While I was flying down this river, I could feel shells hitting my fighter'.

Spears dropped the landing gear, then hurriedly decided to raise it again to prevent the Mustang from falling undamaged into enemy hands. After the badly damaged P-51 had finally slid to a halt, German troops drove up to the fighter and duly captured Spears, but 'They seemed to be trying to be as nice as they could', he said. 'If they had a name badge, they'd shove it right under my nose so I wouldn't miss it. They knew that the war was coming to an end, so they did not want to be involved in any war crimes or any cruelty'.

The Germans gave Spears a half-hearted interrogation. 'They knew full well that any information they got would be useless to them', he said. After just three days in captivity, Spears heard a commotion outside. 'I pulled a board off a window and the first thing I saw was this huge Russian tank'. Soviet troops were firing into buildings at random, so Spears began shouting and waving at them to avoid being hit. One Soviet soldier heard him above the din of battle. 'I had an A-2 flying jacket on with a large American flag on the back. I put my back to the window so he could see it. I heard him yell, 'American! American!' He rushed up and gave me a big bear hug!' Spears subsequently returned to the group on 10 May.

James T Mitchell, who had stayed with Spears as he headed for Polish territory, had landed on the Soviet side for the frontline, while Arnett Starks had been killed in action near Berlin. Armour McDaniel, who had assumed command when Col Davis' P-51 acted up, was forced to bail out when his own Mustang suffered engine trouble, and he ended the war as a PoW. Capt Walter M Downs was appointed to lead the 301st in his absence.

On their way home from the German capital, the group strafed rail traffic, claiming two locomotives and three goods wagons damaged. Gen Lawrence of the 5th BW sent a telegram thanking the group for its extraordinary efforts on the Berlin mission, which resulted in the 332nd being awarded a Distinguished Unit Citation. The latter was awarded to units of the Armed Forces of the United States and its allies for extraordinary heroism in action against an armed enemy.

25 March saw the group conduct a photo-escort for an F-5 overflying Linz, and this was followed up by a 39-aeroplane escort of the 49th BW to Prague/Kbely airfield under the leadership of Capt Jack Holsclaw. Whilst in the target area, the group spotted a Soviet Pe-2 bomber, which rocked its wings as it flew below the American formation. The group manoeuvred to avoid the Russian aircraft, but then watched in horror as two P-51Ds from another unit swooped in and opened fire. The Pe-2 caught fire and dived into the ground.

Hannibal Cox led the next day's F-5 escort to Munich, which was followed by an escort of the 5th BW to the Weiner Neustadt railway marshalling yards. The bombers were forced off course by weather, but they rendezvoused with the 332nd over the target area and were safely shepherded home.

Weather kept the group grounded until 30 March, when Holsclaw led the morning's photo run to Munich. Cloud prevented the F-5 from getting any good photographs, however.

MORE AERIAL VICTORIES

The last day of March 1945 would bring the 332nd its biggest haul of aerial kills in World War 2. With Col Davis in the lead aircraft, 47 Mustangs conducted a fighter sweep of the Munich area, followed by a strafing mission against rail targets. Four aborts brought the number of P-51s to enter German airspace down to 43, and Davis ordered the squadron formations to cover equal thirds of the target area.

Just after the three squadrons split up to look for things to strafe, five Bf 109s and a single Fw 190 suddenly broke out of a cloud bank above a flight of seven Mustangs from the 99th. The pilots, which were in the process of lining up targets to strafe, broke off their attack and engaged the fighters instead. The Fw 190 fell to the guns of 2Lt Thomas Braswell, while the Bf 109s were downed by Maj William Campbell, 1Lt Daniel Rich and 2Lts John Davis, James Hall and Hugh White.

Five minutes later, pilots from the 100th spotted eight Fw 190s and three Bf 109s at 3000 ft. Although these aeroplanes engaged the Mustangs with some aggression, their tactics were haphazard and they failed to allow the German pilots to work as a team. The 100th took full advantage of this.

'I dived into a group of enemy aircraft', reported Robert Williams, who turned onto the tail of one of the Fw 190s. 'I shot off a few short bursts. My fire hit the mark and the enemy aeroplane fell off and tumbled to the ground. On pulling away from my victim, I found another enemy aeroplane on my tail. To evade his guns, I made a steep turn. Just as I had turned, another enemy fighter shot across the nose of my aeroplane. Immediately, I began firing at him'. Williams' aim was true, for the Focke-Wulf went into a steep dive and crashed.

While Williams was engaged, 1Lt Roscoe Brown and 2Lts Bertram Wilson and Rual Bell each despatched a Bf 109, while 1Lt Earl Lane and Flt Off John Lyle downed an Fw 190 apiece.

After dealing with the German fighters, the group resumed its strafing mission. The 99th FS destroyed two locomotives and damaged a third one, whilst 15 passenger carriages were also shot up. In the process, however, Clarence Driver was brought down – he bailed out within view of several of his fellow Tuskegee airmen in Stalag Luft VIIA, located in nearby Moosberg. The burned 'Red' Driver soon joined his friends in the PoW camp.

On its strafing runs, the 301st destroyed three locomotives, two goods wagons and a house, and damaged nine locomotives, 14 goods wagons, six passenger carriages, five oil wagons, five hopper cars, a factory, a railway roundhouse, a railway station and a truck. Meanwhile, the 100th destroyed two locomotives, eight oil wagons, three passenger carriages and a warehouse, while damaging a locomotive, two tank cars, a truck and ten goods wagons. The squadron lost 2Lt Ronald Reeves over the target area when his fighter went into a spin while making a tight turn – he was too low to recover and died in the crash. A second Mustang ran low on gas and went missing during the return flight.

Col Davis and Capt Turner chat with 1Lt Spurgeon Ellington (extreme right) and his crew chief in front of the latter's 100th FS P-51D-15 44-15648 *LOLLIPOOP II* in late 1944 (*Jon Lake Collection*)

April Fools' Day 1945 saw 45 Mustangs rendezvous with the 47th BW's B-24s for a mission to the railway marshalling yards at St Polten, in Austria. Eight fighters from the 301st, led by Lt Harder, preceded the bombers through the target area before turning west and conducting a fighter sweep around Wels and Linz. This flight spotted four Fw 190s below them in the neighbourhood of Wels airfield and dived to the attack. The four low aircraft were bait, as there were two other Fw 190s trailing the first four, with an additional ten Fw 190s and Bf 109s positioned above the six low aircraft to spring the trap. A series of swirling dogfights ensued, with the Germans trying virtually everything to beat the Mustang pilots – head-on passes, Lufberys, turning attacks, deflection shots.

Despite the German aggressiveness, the 301st came out on top in most engagements, with Harry Stewart bagging three Fw 190s and Charles White a pair of Bf 109s. Single kills went to Carl Carey, John Edwards, Walter Manning, Harold Morris and James Fischer. The latter pilot's aeroplane was shot up when he chased his victim across an airfield, and while struggling to bring the Mustang home, he took another shell through the wing over a small town in Yugoslavia which forced him to bail out, although he landed among friendly partisans. Manning was shot down after he scored his kill, as was Flt Off William Armstrong. Both pilots were killed.

The 1 April photo-escort to Prague was uneventful, but the next day's trip to Munich, featuring an F-5 and four 99th P-51s led by Lt Hannibal Cox, had just arrived in the target when the formation was jumped by a lone Me 262, which made a single pass from 'seven o'clock high'. The

Mustangs turned into the Me 262, but the F-5 failed to drop into the No 3 position in the formation as briefed and continued towards Regensburg. While on the way home, two Mustangs gave chase to an Fw 190, but they failed to catch the German aeroplane. Without a Lightning to escort, Cox led the P-51s down to the deck and strafed six river barges during the trip back to Ramitelli.

The mission for 2 April called for an escort of the 304th BW to the railway marshalling yard at Krems, followed by a fighter sweep by the 99th of the area west of Vienna. All 47 Mustangs returned safely. After a short break, the group was up again on 5 April, taking an F-5 to Linz in the morning and shepherding the 5th BW to Udine airfield in the afternoon. The anticipated Luftwaffe response from the latter base never materialised.

On 6 April, the 304th BW attacked the railway marshalling yards at Verona and Porta Nuova, and 39 of the 332nd's Mustangs went with them, led by now-Maj Andrew Turner. No enemy aircraft were spotted, nor were they during the afternoon's photo-recon escort to Prague. The next day, six groups from the 5th BW attacked bridges in northern Italy, and the 332nd provided cover. One aircraft, flown by 2Lt William Walker of the 100th, landed at Zara, in Yugoslavia, and the pilot and P-51 returned to Ramitelli two days later.

The escorting of photo-reconnaissance missions continued to occupy pilots who were not assigned to protect bomber formations. On 7 April, Lt Gentry Barnes led the escort of an F-5 to Munich, and the next day's missions took six-aeroplane escorts to Linz and Munich with a Mosquito and to Prague with a Lightning.

Hannibal Cox led the 34-aeroplane bomber escort mission flown on 8 April as three groups of the 5th BW flattened the railway bridge at Campodazzo. No flak or fighters were seen, although one B-17 was spotted ditching in the Adriatic Sea.

On 9 April, a six-aeroplane escort for an F-5 to Prague, led by Lt Carl Ellis, saw evidence of the Luftwaffe's presence, but never had a chance to engage. During the approach to Prague, 16 twin-engined aircraft were seen on the deck, along with a half-dozen single-engined fighters at about the same time, and 45 minutes later a single Me 262 flew past the formation on a parallel course. A second photo-escort that afternoon to Prague found no sign of these enemy aircraft.

Col Davis led the day's big mission – a 39-aeroplane escort of groups from the 5th and 304th BWs to Bologna. The mission was notable in that there were no aborts, which was a tribute to the groundcrews who had worked hard to master the Mustang.

Bologna was the next day's target as well, with Lt Chris Newman commanding the 34-aeroplane escort. 10 April also saw yet another uneventful photo-recon escort to Munich. The next day, 35 Mustangs covered the 304th BW's attack on the railway bridge at Ponte Gardena – a mission that required the detachment of four P-51s to chaperone a pair of crippled B-24s to safety.

Jack Holsclaw led the escort of an F-5 to Munich on 11 April, seeing no sign of enemy aerial resistance. Two uneventful escorts the next day, to Linz and Munich, were followed by a mission for the 100th and elements of the 301st to escort the 47th BW to the Casara railway bridge, and the

99th and the rest of the 301st to take the 49th BW to St Veith, in Germany. During the latter mission, tragedy struck when 2Lts Samuel Leftenant and James L Hall Jnr collided. Leftenant was killed, although his aeroplane was seen to continue flying south, seemingly under control. Hall bailed out of his damaged P-51 and was captured by the Germans in Rumania – he would rejoin the group after war's end.

On 14 April, Lt Robert Williams led the F-5 escort to Munich and Lake Cheim, and a second six-aeroplane escort provided cover to supply-dropping Halifaxes later that morning.

15 April was a busy day, beginning with F-5 escorts to Bolzano, Prague and Munich. Next came a 29-aeroplane escort of the 304th BW to the Ghedi ammunition factory and storage area. Other than the repeated hostile response of some P-38s to a lone Mustang's efforts to join up with them, the mission was wholly unremarkable.

That same day, Col Davis led 37 P-51Ds on a strafing mission against rail targets in the Munich, Salzburg, Linz, Prague and Regensburg areas – the three squadrons split up and attacked targets in pre-assigned locations. Despite flak from two trains that they harassed, the Mustangs strafed the railway lines unmolested for over an hour. A dozen Mustangs from the 99th destroyed four locomotives and damaged four more. Fourteen goods wagons, four motor transports on flat cars and two railway buildings were also damaged. Flak guns mounted on flat cars peppered Flt Off Thurston Gaines's P-51, forcing him to bail out near Munich – he quickly became a PoW.

A dozen P-51s from the 100th strafed the railway line from Plattling to Passan to Klatovy, destroying five locomotives and damaging four more, as well as five goods wagons cars, a passenger carriage and a house near the tracks.

The 301st had the most interesting time of it. First, their Mustangs strafed river traffic, damaging two barges, a steam crane and a house near the river, then they attacked a railway line, destroying an oil wagon and damaging six others. Four 301st P-51s dropped down from flying top cover and attacked a second railway line, destroying three locomotives and eight oil wagons and damaging a flat car and a goods wagon. The four Mustangs made another pass and claimed four locomotives destroyed and 15 goods wagons, nine locomotives and a passenger carriage damaged, and they also shot up a gun emplacement.

As they pulled off this run, Jimmy Lanham and his wingman spotted a Bf 109 painted dark blue, and lacking German markings – a possible Italian ANR holdout. The Bf 109 tried to turn inside the speeding Mustangs, but Lanham fired a series of deflection shots and saw hits around the cowling. The fighter burst into flames and hit the ground – inexplicably, Lanham was subsequently credited with only a probable victory. On the way home, Flt Off Morris Gant radioed that he was low on fuel, and he was ordered to land at the nearest airfield as the group passed Ortona, in Italy. Gant was never seen again.

16 April continued the hectic pace. Lt Henry Peoples led a four-ship escort of three C-47s to Yugoslavia, and small groups of Mustangs flew three photo-reconnaissance escort missions to the Munich area. A 37-aircraft escort of the 49th and 55th BWs to Bologna took place in the early afternoon. The next day's F-5 escort to Linz and Munich was followed by

a 49-aeroplane effort escorting the 5th and 304th BWs to Bologna. This mission was repeated the next day by 38 Mustangs under Maj Gleed, which took the 304th back to its Italian target. The fighters were supposed to cover the 5th BW, but confusion surrounding the rendezvous time left the 332nd with no one to escort, so Gleed led them to the assistance of the 304th's B-24s.

Col Davis led the mission of 19 April, when 47 P-51s 'rode herd' on the 304th BW, which split into two groups and attacked railway marshalling yards at Wels and Pucheim. Davis put 19 aeroplanes over Wels and 16 over Pucheim, with the last seven set free to conduct a fighter sweep. Unfortunately, no fighters could be seen in the air, but as the pilots were preparing to climb back to altitude, they encountered the astounding site of 35 to 40 Me 163 rocket aircraft piled together in a large pasture – mute evidence of the effects of the Allies' bombing campaign on German industry. Six Mustangs also accompanied an F-5 Lightning to Munich that morning.

On 20 April, two groups of 25 aircraft left Ramitelli 49 minutes apart to cover penetration, target cover and withdrawal of 49th BW 'heavies' attacking the Lusia railway bridge and the 55th BW's attacks on the Boara and Gazare railway bridges in northern Italy. Despite delays on the part of the bombers, the mission went without a hitch. Jimmy Lanham led the similarly-smooth F-5 escort to Prague.

That afternoon, Col Davis received a letter from Wendell Pruitt in which he pleaded him to allow him come back to combat. Pruitt was now at Tuskegee as an instructor, a job that he had little patience for. Ironically, the very day his request arrived at Ramitelli, Pruitt and a student were performing a low-altitude roll when the aeroplane fell out of the sky and smashed into a field. Pruitt, the survivor of 70 combat missions, and his student were both killed.

The following morning, 23 aircraft from the 99th and 301st were assigned to escort the 49th BW to the Attang/Pucheim railway marshalling yards. Because of poor weather, the group never rendezvoused with the bombers during their approach to the target, but it was able to pick them up coming off the bomb run on the second alternate target. 2Lt Leland Pennington's P-51 left the formation en route to the rendezvous near Zara and, foregoing an escort, proceeded home alone. Pennington never made it, and he was later classified as killed in action.

Capt Emile Clifton led a second mission that day – a 25-aeroplane fighter sweep of the Udine area. Initially, the Mustangs were tasked with attacking an area around Augsburg and Munich, but a wall of cloud prevented them from getting too far north. The group also squeezed in another escort of a Lancaster and a Halifax as they dropped supplies to partisans in Yugoslavia.

After an aborted photo-reconnaissance mission on the morning of 22 April, 32 Mustangs of the 99th and 100th FSs carried out an armed reconnaissance between Stanghella, Monselice, Padova, Nogara, Verona and Nantova, in northern Italy. The 100th encountered weather that prohibited it from hunting for targets, but ten P-51s from the 99th completed their mission. The unit claimed a passenger carriage destroyed and eight others damaged. Capt Chaskin, A-3 of XV Fighter Command, flew the mission in the ironically-coded position of 'white leader'.

23 April brought more escort work. Two forces from the 332nd accompanied the 55th and 304th BWs on missions to Padua and Cavarzere, in northern Italy. After completing their escort, 16 aeroplanes of the first force conducted an armed reconnaissance of the areas around Verona, Morostica, Padua, Cavarzare, Staghella and Legnana. Three aircraft strafed a railway line, damaging one car and a small factory. Hugh White was hit by flak at about 1000 ft, but he had enough speed to climb to 4500 ft before bailing out, coming down near Padua, where he was captured. Eventually, with the war's end clearly in sight, his captors surrendered to him! White returned to the group on 6 May 1945. The 332nd also flew two photo-escort missions to Prague and Brno.

Ed Gleed led the first part of the 24 April mission to northern Italy, escorting the 47th and 49th BWs to the Rovereto and San Ambrogio railway bridges. The second element was commanded by 1Lt Gordon Rapier. The German forces failed to so much as fire a single round of flak at either group of attacking aeroplanes.

The next day, the 332nd sent up four eight-aircraft forces on an armed reconnaissance mission in the Verona area. One flight, led by Gentry Barnes, spotted a convoy and made a firing pass, damaging a truck before red crosses were spotted on three or four of the 50 vehicles in the convoy. 25 April also saw three more photo-reconnaissance missions flown, including one led by Lt Rapier to Munich. The six Mustangs and one Mosquito stumbled across a single Fw 190 14,000 ft below them, which immediately 'split-S'ed' away and dived for the deck.

The third mission of the day – an F-5 escort to the Pilsen area led by Lt Leon Turner – was interrupted by the arrival of a lone Me 262, which

The 302nd FS's Luke Weathers (sat on the wing of his second Mustang, named *Beale Street*) poses with groundcrew in early 1945 (*Jon Lake Collection*)

closed on the F-5 from 'six o'clock'. Three of the Mustangs turned to intercept the jet, and they were joined in their pursuit by three P-38s. With the odds against him, the Me 262 broke for home.

LAST AERIAL VICTORIES

With the war winding down, it was apparent that few enemy airmen relished the idea of being the last pilot killed in the service of the Reich. Just the same, the F-5 escort of 26 April resulted in the 332nd's final scores, and the final aerial victories for the Fifteenth Air Force.

Six Mustangs, led by Lt Charles Wilson, escorted an F-5 Lightning to the vicinity of Linz, Prague and Amstetting. At 1205 hrs, 15 miles east of Prague, three of the Mustangs spotted an aircraft and dropped down to investigate. The aeroplane turned out to be a lone Mosquito.

As the Mustangs climbed to rejoin the formation, they stumbled across five Bf 109s, which initially rocked their wings to appear friendly. When the Mustangs broke into them, two Bf 109s pulled up as if to dive. A P-51 pilot fired two bursts at one of the fighters and it spiralled into the ground and exploded. The three other Messerschmitts 'split-S'ed' for the perceived safety of the ground, but two other Mustangs, with their advantage in the dive, despatched two of these Bf 109s, one of whose pilots bailed out. The remaining fighters were caught after a short chase, and one was promptly destroyed while the other was claimed as a probable. Thomas Jefferson scored one kill and the probable and Jimmy Lanham, William Price and Richard Simmons each bagged a fighter apiece.

That same day, Col Davis led a complicated five-part escort for the 47th and 55th BWs to the Casarsa and Malcontenta ammunition dumps. The 332nd had fighters over the bombers for two-and-a-half hours, having staggered take-off times to ensure coverage of the bomber stream.

30 April saw a fitting end to the 332nd's war. Lt Herbert Barland led a four-aeroplane escort of an F-5 to Balzano, in Italy, which went entirely without incident.

With the war's end a few days later, the group moved to a much more comfortable field at Cattolica, and participated in the Fifteenth Air Force Review over Caserta and Bari on 6 May. While preparing for a return to the US and a possible redeployment to the Pacific, there was a simmering pride in the men at their achievements. The 99th FS and the 332nd FG had destroyed 111 aircraft in the air and 150 on the ground, wrecked 57 locomotives, damaged or destroyed more than 600 goods wagons and flown 15,533 sorties. Moreover, as far as anyone could determine, they had never lost a bomber under escort to enemy aircraft.

The latter claim is hard to verify, for although mission reports do not mention the loss of any aircraft under escort, it is all but impossible to determine which groups the 332nd was covering at specific times. Even Col Davis expressed uncertainty about this now-famous claim. 'I don't say that, or if I do say it, it's not an over-enthusiastic statement. I question that privately', he told USAF historian Alan Gropman in 1990. 'But so many people have said it that a lot of people have come to believe it'.

The most important believers in the 332nd's claim were the bomber crews of the Fifteenth Air Force, many of whose veterans to this day proclaim that the most beautiful things they ever saw in the skies of southern Europe were the red-tailed Mustangs of the 332nd FG.

LOCKBOURNE AND THE END

On 8 June 1945, the group held a ceremony at Cattolica during which Col Davis was awarded the Silver Star for his leadership during the 15 April mission. Within hours of the ceremony, Davis and a cadre of 40 officers and airmen were on B-17s on the first leg of their return trip to the USA. Their task was to rebuild the 477th Medium Bombardment Group, which would be merged with the 332nd FG to become the 477th Composite Group (Coloured).

The 477th was subsequently bounced from base to base – far worse, it was the victim of overt racism that kept it from becoming a deployable unit. The slights ranged from substandard facilities to exclusion from the PX and officers' club, to the outright hostility of Gen Frank O D Hunter, commander of the First Air Force. 'As long as I am commander of the First Air Force, there will be no racial mixing at any post under my command', Hunter proclaimed in 1944.

Col Robert Selway, who was the white CO of the 477th, helped enforce Hunter's prejudicial policies. Upon arrival at Freeman Field, in Indiana, Selway divided the officers' clubs along racial lines. In an effort to disguise this, he said Club No 1 was open to 'trainees', which was how all black officers were classified at Freeman Field, and Club No 2 was open to instructors and supervisors. The men of the 477th made plans to 'integrate' Club No 2, and on 5 April 1945, Lts Marsden Thompson and Shirley Clinton entered the club and were arrested. Next came Roger Terry. Throughout the next day, 58 more black airmen tried to exercise their rights as officers, only to be taken into custody by white MPs.

On 9 April, Selway ordered the black officers to sign a statement that they understood his orders regulating segregation of the officers' clubs.

By February 1946, the 477th Composite Group had just a dozen P-47Ns on strength. The Thunderbolts had the fronts of their cowls and the tips of their vertical stabilisers painted red, with a large white block aircraft letter atop the tail (*National Air and Space Museum*)

101 officers refused to sign, and they were bundled off to Godman Field on 13 April.

Selway's belief that he had quelled the rebellion was toppled the next day when he learned that every black officer left at Freeman Field planned to enter the club that night. Selway closed the club, the 101 non-signers were released, and only the original three entrants to the club were held in custody. They were submitted to a court martial, which concluded by fining Terry $150 for forcing past an MP at the club door. In the 1990s, an official order dismissed charges against all the participants in what became known as 'the Freeman Field Mutiny'.

Following the court martial, Selway was relieved and Davis took over the group on 24 June. For the first time, the group had black officers in responsible positions, namely Ed Gleed as group operations officer, Andrew Turner as deputy group commander and former 332nd flight surgeon Vance Marchbanks as base surgeon, among others. William Campbell assumed command of the newly-attached 99th FS. On 1 July, Davis took charge of Godman Field itself and appointed Lee Rayford as base operations officer.

The group trained for deployment to the Pacific, with the Mustangs being replaced by P-47N Thunderbolts, but the war's end saw the wholesale departure of pilots back to the civilian world and the group shrank accordingly, leaving just 16 B-25H/Js and 12 P-47Ns on strength by February 1946. In March, the group was transferred to Lockbourne Field, near Columbus, Ohio, which became the only all-black base in the Army Air Force.

Their welcome at the airfield underscored how pervasive racism was, even in Ohio. The editor of the Columbus *Citizen* objected to the arrival of the black airmen, insisting that 'this is still a white man's country', and that it was totally unacceptable for America's wars to be fought by 'servants'.

Caught between the hostile members of the community and the 332nd were a group of white civilian employees who feared that they would lose their jobs as a result of the arrival of the black airmen. Col Davis held a meeting for these employees and assured them that as long as they did their jobs they would remain in their roles at the base. 'They became our very great allies and public relations-types with the local people', Davis later said.

Davis also spelled out his expectations of his men. 'I made the statement early on that we were going to make Lockbourne the best base in the Air

A P-47N returns to Lockbourne Air Force Base at the end of a training mission in 1946. The group initially adopted the N-model Thunderbolt when a transfer to the Pacific seemed imminent, and they retained them until the unit's disbandment (*National Air and Space Museum*)

Force', Davis said. 'And, by 1948, in an inspection report, there is a statement that said it could well serve as a model for bases in the Air Force'.

In May 1947, the 477th reverted to being the 332nd FG after disposing of its B-25s. Three months later, the group became the 332nd Fighter Wing, and shrank even further in size. The segregated nature of the USAAF meant that there was little room for advancement for black officers and enlisted men. Instead of competing for promotions against all others in their specialities, the men competed against all black men in their area — in other words, the men they worked with at Lockbourne.

After two years of this, there was a light at the end of the tunnel – President Harry S Truman, engaged in the difficult 1948 election campaign, decreed that the armed services of the USA would provide 'equality and opportunity for all persons without regard to race, colour, religion or national origin'.

It would take a while, but segregation in the US military was soon to be a thing of the past due in large part to the outstanding wartime exploits of the 332nd FG.

In the meantime, the unit continued to fly training missions. On 28 March 1948, a five-ship formation took off from Shaw Air Force Base in Greenville, South Carolina, on a simulated armed reconnaissance. The final destination of this flight would be Lockbourne for four of the pilots, but Harry Stewart would not be among them.

'We were flying in formation over Eastern Kentucky, passing through a thunderstorm, when I had engine failure at 20,000 ft', he said. 'I rode the aeroplane down to 10,000 ft, but I was still in the clouds, and I knew there were mountains in the area'.

Rather than risking an unexpected rendezvous with a mountaintop, Stewart, a veteran of 43 wartime missions, elected to bail out. He opened the canopy, unbuckled his seat belt, and 'trimmed the nose forward so that when I let go of the stick, the nose would dip and eject me forward', he explained. 'Unfortunately, the slipstream hit me and I flew back, hitting my left leg on the tail of the aeroplane, breaking it in two places between the calf and ankle'.

Harry Stewart scored three kills in one day on 1 April 1945, and remained in the Army Air Force after war's end. His biggest scare came in 1948 when his P-47N's engine failed and he was badly injured during his bail out (*National Museum of the USAF*)

While the injured Stewart floated down over the Kentucky coal mining town of Van Lear, his P-47N hurtled over the Webb family cemetery and crashed into a hilltop overlooking the home of the soon-to-be-famous country singer Loretta Lynn, exploding and leaving a crater ten to fifteen feet deep.

'I'd lost my shoe on the leg I broke, which was bleeding profusely', Stewart said. 'I must have been in shock, because I remember wondering why I had got up that morning and put on one red sock and one brown one'. He used his white silk flying scarf to improvise a tourniquet for his bleeding leg. Then he began to wonder

119

The 332nd's team in the 1949
USAF Gunnery Meet – Alva Temple,
Harry Stewart, James Harvey
and alternate Halbert Alexander
(*National Museum of the USAF*)

how he was going to save himself. 'Just then, I heard a voice from afar, yelling out, "Hello, hello!"' Stewart said. 'Of course, I replied with a frantic "Hello!" of my own. I didn't want to take a chance on them not hearing me'.

A man named Lafe Daniels found Stewart beneath a rock cliff and loaded him onto his horse. Daniels took the aviator home to his wife, Mary, who cleaned and bandaged his wounds. To treat Stewart's pain, the Daniels employed a clear, all-purpose mountain remedy that Stewart mistook for water. Daniels then took the pilot to a clinic in nearby Paintsville. The doctors gave him morphine for his pain, Stewart said, and 'the combination of moonshine and morphine put me in another world'.

'I remember people lined up outside the door to see this apparition', Stewart said. 'The mayor came in and introduced himself', he said, 'followed by the police chief, county sheriff and a reporter from *The Paintsville Herald*.' Tellingly, the story in the local paper about the crash did not mention that the pilot was black.

Stewart's Thunderbolt became an item of interest for the community as well. By the time Air Force officials showed up to investigate the crash site,

nearly every scrap of the wreckage was gone. The locals picked up what they could find – Stewart's cap, machine gun rounds, even the propeller, which one witness said was last seen lashed to the side of a Jeep owned by Loretta Lynn's husband. Eventually, residents hitched three mules to the wreckage and hauled the entire aeroplane off the hill and onto a cattle truck. The P-47's carcass was taken to Ashland, where it was sold as scrap for $70. Once his broken leg had healed, Stewart returned to active duty.

In May 1949, the newly-established US Air Force held its first continental gunnery meet, with teams from every fighter group in the country congregating at Las Vegas Air Force Base. The 332nd team was made up of Stewart, Alva Temple and James Harvey. These veterans competed against other pilots in six categories – air-to-air gunnery at 10,000 ft and 20,000 ft, rocket-firing, skip-bombing, dive-bombing and strafing. Each team's scores in these events would be averaged out to determine a winner.

In the skip-bombing phase, each man scored a hit in all six passes for a perfect score. In the rocket-firing competition, Temple scored hits with eight of eight, while Stewart and Harvey scored seven of eight. The competition continued in this vein until the trio compiled the best score as a team for 'conventionally-powered' aircraft, with Temple finishing second in individual scores. About a month later, perhaps not coincidentally, the 332nd FG was disbanded and its personnel transferred to various commands within the Air Force.

For many, the idea of leaving an all-black unit was daunting, but Col Davis was convinced that desegregation was the only way to cement the progress his units had made. 'I told them that when you join those units, you're going to outshine them', he said. 'That's exactly the way it turned out. They were far in advance of their contemporaries in the white units. They had the combat experience, they had the flying background and they had the knowledge. What more is there?'

A P-47N pulls off a bombing run after putting a hole in the target during the skip-bombing phase of the competition. The 332nd team took first place – a feat which electrified Lockbourne AFB. However, the trophy for the competition win disappeared while the group was being deactivated, and Air Force records neglected to mention the group's victory for many years (*National Museum of the USAF*)

APPENDICES

APPENDIX 1

AERIAL VICTORIES OF THE 99th FS and 332nd FG

	Kills	Probables	Damaged	Types (total)
99th FS	34	5.5	13	Fw 190 (20), Bf 109 (13), C.205 (1)
100th FS	24	0	2	Bf 109 (15), Fw 190 (5), Me 262 (3), Re.2001 (1)
301st FS	32	2	6	Bf 109 (22) Fw 190 (10)
302nd FS	29	1	6	Bf 109 (23) Fw 190 (2) He 111 (3) C.205 (1)
Total	**119**	**8.5**	**27**	Bf 109 (73) Fw 190 (37) Me 262 (3) He 111 (3) C.205 (2) Re.2001 (1)

APPENDIX 2

PILOTS WITH MULTIPLE CONFIRMED AERIAL KILLS

Lee Archer, 302nd	5 (5 Bf 109s)	Carl Carey, 301st	2 (2 Bf 109s)
Edward Toppins, 99th	4 (2 Bf 109s and 2 Fw 190s)	Robert Diez, 99th	2 (2 Fw 190s)
Joseph Elsberry, 301st	4 (3 Fw 109s and 1 Bf 109)	Wilson Eagleson, 99th	2 (2 Fw 190s)
Charles Hall, 99th	3 (2 Fw 190s and 1 Bf 109)	John Edwards, 301st	2 (2 Bf 109s)
Wendell Pruitt, 302nd	3 (2 Bf 109s and 1 He 111)	Frederick Funderburg, 301st	2 (2 Bf 109s)
Roger Romine, 302nd	3 (3 Bf 109s)	Edward Gleed, 302nd	2 (2 Fw 190s)
Leonard Jackson, 99th	3 (2 Bf 109s and 1 Fw 190)	Alfred Gorham, 301st	2 (2 Fw 190s)
Clarence Lester, 100th	3 (3 Bf 109s)	Jack Holsclaw, 100th	2 (2 Bf 109s)
Harry Stewart, 301st	3 (3 Bf 109s)	Thomas Jefferson, 301st	2 (2 Bf 109s)
William Green, 302nd	2.5 (1 C.205, 1 He 111 and 0.5 Bf 109)	Jimmy Lanham, 301st	2 (2 Bf 109s)
		Luther Smith, 302nd	2 (1 Bf 109 and1 He 111)
Luke Weathers, 302nd	2.5 (2.5 Bf 109s)	Charles White, 301st	2 (2 Bf 109s)
Roscoe Brown, 100th	2 (1 Me 262 and 1 Bf 109)	Robert Williams, 301st	2 (2 Fw 190s)

COLOUR PLATES

1

AT-6A 41-6058, Tuskegee Army Air Field, 1942

Wearing early-war colours, this AT-6A Texan graced the cover of the 1942 Yearbook of the Tuskegee Army Air Field Flying School. The TU prefix in the aircraft's fuselage identifying code denoted the AT-6's assignment to Tuskegee Army Air Field. The base operated a fleet of PT-13 Kaydets, PT-19 Cornells, BT-13 'Vibrators' and AT-6 Texans for its students, with a mix of twin-engined types for multi-engined and navigation training. Unlike many training command Texans, this particular aircraft survived the war and was finally scrapped at Craig Army Air Field in late 1945.

2

P-40L-5 42-10448 *A TRAIN II* of 1Lt Charles Dryden, 99th FS, Fardjouna, Tunisia, June 1944

A replacement for his first *A TRAIN*, Dryden's P-40L was picked up fresh from the depot at Oujda before it could receive RAF-style camouflage. *A TRAIN II* carried Dryden safely through 30 missions, including the 99th's first aerial tangle with German fighters, before he was rotated home to serve as an instructor. Before Dryden could leave Tunisia, however, he witnessed Sidney Brooks belly-land this aircraft. Although Brooks escaped from the burning wreck, he later died of secondary shock. Dryden stayed in the Army Air Force after war's end, and later flew as a T-6 'Mosquito' spotter pilot in the Korean War, before retiring as a colonel in 1962.

3

P-40L-15 42-10888 *ACE OF PEARLS* of 2Lt Herman 'Ace' Lawson, 99th FS, Madna, Italy, December 1943

Lawson, who arrived among the second group of replacement pilots sent to the 99th FS, survived two engine failures in P-40s, one of which deposited him in the Mediterranean Sea, before taking *ACE OF PEARLS* as his own aircraft. Lawson remained in combat for 18 months, eventually flying a P-51B that was also called *ACE OF PEARLS*. A photographer for Fresno State University in California before the war, Lawson was so eager to become a pilot that upon getting his orders to flight school in the mail, he drove to the local train station and abandoned his car – with more $1000 worth of camera equipment in the trunk – to board a train that was bound for Tuskegee Army Air Field.

4

P-40L-10 42-10841 *NONA II* of 2Lt Alva Temple, 99th FS, Madna, Italy, November 1943

Shortly after arriving as a replacement in the squadron, Alabama native Temple took off as part of a ground-attack mission but clipped his gear on a fence at the end of the runway. Although one undercarriage leg refused to retract fully, Temple completed the mission and then belly-landed *NONA II* back at Madna, badly damaging the aeroplane's left wing in the process. Having survived 120 missions, Temple remained with the group post-war and duly became a key member of the legendary team that won the May 1949 All-Air Force Gunnery Meet at Las Vegas Air Force Base.

5

P-40L-15 42-10461 *JOSEPHINE* of 1Lt Charles Bailey, 99th FS, Madna, Italy, January 1944

During the 99th's second mission on 27 January 1944, Bailey used this machine to destroy an Fw 190. Its markings are an unusual mix, including an RAF fin flash, stars and bars on the wings and a disc and star without bars on the fuselage. In two missions on this day, the squadron destroyed eight, damaged two and tallied two probables.

6

P-40L-15 42-10855 of 1Lt Robert W Diez, 99th FS, Madna, Italy, January 1944

During the morning mission on 27 January 1944, Diez was startled to see an Fw 190 flying a parallel course 750 ft off the wing of 42-10855, oblivious to his presence. The former Oregon University track star slid behind the fighter and shot it down. Two days later Diez managed to score his second kill (again in 42-10855), which was also a Focke-Wulf fighter.

7

P-39Q-20 44-3028 *QUANTO COSTA* of 1Lt Samuel Curtis, 100th FS, Capodichino, Italy, May 1944

The recipient of worn out examples of fighter aircraft utterly unsuited to combat in the Mediterranean Theatre, the 332nd FG first went to war in hand-me-downs like the suggestively named *QUANTO COSTA*, which wears nose art from its previous assignment, probably with the 350th FG. Samuel Curtis flew this veteran Airacobra on a series of fruitless harbour patrol missions from Capodichino during the spring of 1944.

8

P-47D (serial unknown) of 1Lt Gwynne Peirson, Ramitelli, 302nd FS, Italy, June 1944

In addition to flying 73 missions, Peirson's place in the 332nd's history books was sealed when gunfire from his P-47D triggered the explosion that sank the German-crewed Italian minelayer TA-27 in Trieste Harbour. He and wingman Wendell Pruitt were awarded the Distinguished Flying Cross in the wake of this mission. Peirson, a native of Oakland, California, had survived a crash-landing in another P-47 in early June.

9

P-47D-16 42-75971 of 2Lt Lloyd Hathcock, 301st FS, Ramitelli, Italy, May 1944

One of the first Thunderbolts received by the 332nd, this aircraft had previously been the mount of eight-kill ace George Novotny from the 317th FS/325th FG. Hathcock became disoriented during a mission on 29 May 1944 and landed in Rome, where he and his aircraft were captured. The aeroplane was given a yellow cowling and undersides, coded T9+LK and flown north to Rechlin, in Germany, for testing.

10

P-47D-22 (serial, pilot and unit unknown), Ramitelli, Italy, June 1944

The group's hand-me-downs were often pressed into service quickly, and this aircraft is one of the best examples of this practice. The red tail of the 332nd was applied over the markings of the 57th FG, although the latter group's yellow band on the vertical fin was retained. The logo on the cowling belonged to its previous owner, the 64th FS 'Black Scorpions'.

11

P-51C-10 (serial unknown) *"INA THE MACON BELLE"* of Lt Lee Archer Jnr, 302nd FS, Ramitelli, Italy, July 1944
Archer used *"INA THE MACON BELLE"* to become the only officially-recognised black ace in US history, this honour only being bestowed on him in the early 1990s after an Air Force review of kill claims. In an effort to avoid the publicity associated with the first black ace, the USAAF had changed the classification of Archer's first victim – a Bf 109, downed on 19 July 1944 – to a half-kill after it was discovered that his wingman, Freddie Hutchins, had also fired a burst at the Messerschmitt after the fighter's left wing had disintegrated. The review five decades later restored the full kill, giving Archer five victories, and official ace status. Archer and wingman Wendell Pruitt proved to be the 332nd's most lethal pair, with Pruitt knocking down three aircraft. The pair also indulged in post-mission victory rolls until they executed rolls in opposing directions after a mission in October 1944 which almost resulted in a mid-air collision! This would have proven an ironic twist on the team's nickname of 'the Gruesome Twosome'.

12

P-51C (serial unknown) *Joedebelle* of Capt Joseph Elsberry, 301st FS, Ramitelli, Italy, July 1944
While flying this aircraft, Capt 'Jodie' Elsberry scored three kills and a probable on 12 July 1944 over southern France – all of them Fw 190s. Although other members of Elsberry's flight saw the enemy aircraft crash, these kills do not appear on the official Air Force list of victories, however. On 19 July, Elsberry despatched a Bf 109 to run his score to four, plus a probable, leaving him just one short of ace status. After the war, Elsberry remained in the Air Force, rising to the rank of major, but the pressures of racism eventually contributed to a drinking problem that cut his life short.

13

P-51B/C (serial unknown) *TOPPER III* of Capt Edward Toppins, 99th FS, Ramitelli, Italy, August 1944
One of the first replacements to join the 99th FS, Ed Toppins was described as a 'pilot's pilot' and 'almost a daredevil' by his fellow aviators. With four kills, he was the second-highest scorer in the group. This aircraft was issued to Toppins after he had scored his fourth kill. One of his earlier *TOPPER*s had to be scrapped after he warped its fuselage diving on an enemy aircraft (which he destroyed). Following his tour, Toppins married the widow of Sidney Brooks, but he was himself killed in the crash of P-40N 44-7754 at Tuskegee Army Air Field on 17 March 1945.

14

P-51B/C (serial unknown) *ALICE-JO* of Capt Wendell Pruitt, 302nd FS, Ramitelli, Italy, September 1944
Considered by many of his fellow pilots as the 'best stick' in the 332nd, Pruitt used *ALICE-JO* to down three enemy

aircraft (two Bf 109s and an He 111). His earlier exploits included participating in the sinking of a German minelayer. Even so, he was a soft-spoken man on the ground. As a fellow pilot told historian John Holway, 'He only flew loud'. After being rotated home, Pruitt served as an instructor at Tuskegee Army Air Field, which was a task he hated. Before he could wangle a second combat tour in Europe, however, Pruitt and a student were killed when their AT-6 failed to pull out of a roll at low altitude on 20 April 1945.

15

P-51C-10 42-103960 *Skipper's Darlin' III* of Capt Andrew 'Jug' Turner, Ramitelli, Italy, September 1944
Turner, who was the business-like CO of the 100th FS, had taken command of the unit upon the death of Robert Tresville. The son of a Washington minister, Turner graduated in Class 42-I after leaving Howard University and began demonstrating leadership skills that would see him rise to the rank of major before war's end. Sadly, the careful, deliberate, Turner was killed in the post-war crash of a P-47N at Lockbourne Air Force Base on 14 September 1947.

16

P-51C-10 42-103956 *Miss-Pelt* of 1Lt Clarence 'Lucky' Lester, 100th FS, Ramitelli, Italy, September 1944
Lester, from Chicago, Illinois, acquired his nickname from his abilities at poker, but the name was fitting for his combat career as well – in 95 missions, his aeroplane was never so much as scratched by enemy fire. On 18 July, Lester used this fighter to destroy three Bf 109s in the Udine-Treviso area on a day when the group downed 11 enemy aircraft in total. The Mustang had been purchased in part with $75,000 raised by the students and teachers of the Sisters of Notre Dame's Alphonsius School in Chicago. After the war, Lester remained in the Air Force, earned a degree from Stanford University in international relations and served in the Pentagon until finally taking his retirement in 1969. He then founded the Inner City Fund, a venture capital initiative aimed at financing urban businesses.

17

P-51C (serial unknown) *APACHE II* of 1Lt Henry Perry, 99th FS, Ramitelli, Italy, September 1944
The youngest of six children born to a Georgia minister, 'Herky' Perry was a member of Class 42-H at Tuskegee Army Air Field, graduating in September 1942. He was initially assigned to the then-forming 332nd FG, but was plucked from its ranks to join the 99th FS and met up with the squadron in Licata on 22 July 1943. After surviving his early combat experiences in a P-40L, Perry traded his Curtiss fighter for P-51C *APACHE II* when the 99th converted to Mustangs in July 1944. He completed 145 combat missions and, over the course of a 28-year Air Force career, amassed 5500 flying hours before retiring as a colonel in 1970.

18

P-51C (serial unknown) *LUCIFER* of 1Lt Luther Smith, 302nd FS, Ramitelli, Italy, October 1944
Since there were four pilots named Smith among the original members of the 332nd FG, the fast-talking native

of Des Moines, Iowa, was dubbed 'Quibblin' Smith' to differentiate him from the other similarly-surnamed aviators. Smith fired as fast as he talked, being credited with two aerial kills and ten aircraft destroyed on the ground. On his 133rd mission, Smith's *LUCIFER* caught fire after being severely damaged when an ammunition dump exploded below him as he was strafing a freight yard near Lake Balaton, in Hungary. Smith became entangled in the cockpit and escaped only after suffering severe injuries to his ankle and hip. German troops subsequently found him in his parachute, hanging from a tree, and he spent the next seven months in various hospitals until war's end, after which he convalesced for a further two years in Air Force hospitals. Smith was discharged from military service as a captain in 1947.

19

P-51D (serial unknown) *"Little Freddie"* of 1Lt Freddie Hutchins, 302nd FS, Ramitelli, Italy, October 1944
After Hutchins used this Mustang (one of the first P-51Ds issued to the 332nd FG) to destroy four aeroplanes on the ground at Grosswardein airfield on 30 August 1944, *"Little Freddie"* (the second Mustang to bear his name) was destroyed during a strafing mission on 6 October. With flak having disabled the aeroplane, Hutchins was forced to make a high-speed crash-landing that ripped off the fighter's engine, wings and tail. With the help of friendly Greek civilians, Hutchins received first aid and made his way back to Allied forces on 23 October. He duly completed the rest of his tour, flying a further four Mustangs named *"Little Freddie"*.

20

P-51C (serial unknown) *DAISEY MAE* of Capt Woody Crockett, 100th FS, Ramitelli, Italy, November 1944
'Woody' Crockett joined the Army as a private in 1940 and was soon honoured as 'Model Soldier of the Regiment' in the service's first all-black field artillery unit. In time, he was assigned to Class 43-C at Tuskegee Army Air Field and graduated on 25 March 1943. Crockett's 15-month tour with the 100th saw him fly 149 combat missions. His quick actions saved William Hill when two Mustangs collided on take-off at Ramitelli on 16 November 1944, and he was rewarded with the soldier's medal as a result of his bravery on this date. Crockett remained in the Air Force and flew 45 missions in the Korean War, before finally retiring in 1970. The nose art on *DAISEY MAE* was the result of the happy convergence between the names of a character in Al Capp's *Lil' Abner* comic strip and Crockett's wife, the former Daisy Juanita McMurry.

21

P-51C (serial unknown) *By Request* of Col Benjamin O Davis, CO of the 332nd FG, Ramitelli, Italy, December 1944
So-named because of the request for 332nd FG escorts from bomb groups that had become commonplace by mid-1944, the personal aircraft of Benjamin O Davis was rare among group P-51B/Cs in having an extended tail fillet similar to that fitted to most D-model Mustangs. The fighter was written off in a crash at Ramitelli in late December 1944 while Davis was back in the USA enjoying a brief spell of leave.

22

P-51C (serial unknown) *MY BUDDY* of Capt Charles Bailey, 99th FS, Ramitelli, Italy, December 1944
Charles Bailey completed 133 missions with the 99th FS before rotating home to take on training duties at Tuskegee Army Air Field. Bailey and his five brothers served in all four branches of the US military during the war. Following the cessation of hostilities, Bailey returned to his home in Punta Gorda, Florida, and became a teacher.

23

P-51D-15 44-15648 *LOLLIPOOP II* of 1Lt Spurgeon Ellington, 100th FS, Ramitelli, Italy, December 1944
Ellington, a resident of Winston-Salem, South Carolina, before the war, graduated in Class 43-E on 28 May 1943 and shipped out as an original member of the 332nd FG. He flew in the same section as Robert Tresville on the fateful mission of 23 June 1944 during which the latter pilot's P-47D crashed into the ocean while flying at low level. *LOLLIPOOP II* was named for Ellington's wife, Marie. Ellington was subsequently killed in a flying accident in October 1945, and his widow later married singer Nat 'King' Cole.

24

P-51D (serial unknown) *Creamer's Dream* of 1Lt Charles White, 301st FS, Ramitelli, Italy, January 1945
White, who hailed from St Louis, Missouri, joined the 100th FS as a replacement in late 1944. His vociferous protestations about the condition of his first assigned aircraft (a P-51C) resulted in him eventually being given one of the group's first P-51Ds. The artwork applied below the cockpit was presented in a frontal view on the right side of the aeroplane and a rear view on the left side – the images were uniform thanks to the use of a template! White was flying this aircraft when he destroyed two Bf 109s on 1 April 1945.

25

P-51D-15 44-15648 *DUCHESS ARLENE* of 1Lt Robert W Williams, 301st FS, Ramitelli, Italy, March 1945
Robert Williams downed two Fw 190s during his tenure with the 332nd, both during the group's fighter sweep of the Munich area on 30 March 1945 while flying *DUCHESS ARLENE*, which had formerly been Spurgeon Ellington's *LOLLIPOOP II*. Williams, a native of Ottumwa, Iowa, re-named the Mustang in honour of his hometown sweetheart, Arlene Roberts. He flew 50 combat missions before returning to civilian life, where he became an actor, appearing on television with Phil Silvers and Dick Van Dyke, as well as in the film *Pork Chop Hill* with Gregory Peck. Williams later wrote the screenplay for the 1995 HBO film *The Tuskegee Airmen*, starring Laurence Fishburne, Cuba Gooding Jnr and Andre Braugher.

26

P-51D (serial unknown) *TALL in the SADDLE* of 1Lt George Hardy, 99th FS, Ramitelli, Italy, February 1945
George Hardy of Philadelphia, Pennsylvania, arrived in Italy in time to fly 21 missions – most of them in this P-51, adorned with the familiar Vargas pin-up girl. Hardy elected to remain in the Air Force post-war, and flew 45 missions in B-29s over Korea and a further 70 missions over

Vietnam in AC-119K gunships. He eventually retired with the rank of lieutenant colonel.

27

P-51B (serial unknown) *KITTEN* of 2Lt Leon 'Woodie' Spears, 302nd FS, Ramitelli, Italy, March 1945
Taken on as a replacement for his first P-51B 42-103968 *Donna*, 'Woodie' Spears' *KITTEN* had already carried Charles McGee through a 136-mission tour. '"Kitten" was my wife's nickname', McGee explained, 'but also my crew chief, Nathaniel Wilson, kept that engine purring like a contented kitten'. McGee would fly Mustangs (also named *KITTEN*) in Korea, and then flew RF-4 Phantom IIs as commander of the 16th Tactical Reconnaissance Squadron in Vietnam, amassing 408 combat missions over the course of his 31-year career. Spears' tenure in the military was shorter – he was hit by heavy flak over Berlin during

the 332nd's Distinguished Unit Citation-winning mission of 23 March 1945. With part of its wing sheared off, Spears coaxed *KITTEN* to a wheels-up landing in Poland, where he was briefly held as a PoW before his captors were overrun by the Soviets. The first *KITTEN* ended its proud career in a Polish scrapyard.

28

P-51D (serial unknown) *MEATBALL RAP II* of Flt Off Charles Lane, 99th FS, Ramitelli, Italy, March 1945
Lane graduated from training at TAAF in 1944 and flew 26 combat missions, most of them in Mustangs named *MEATBALL RAP*. He remained in the Air Force after the war and flew fighters, transports and B-52s before taking retirement in 1970. Lane then devoted 22 years to the anti-poverty programme Greater Omah a Community Action.

INDEX

References to illustrations are shown in **bold**. Plates are shown with page and caption locators in (brackets).